Florence Nightingale

Twayne's English Authors Series

Herbert Sussman, Editor
Northeastern University

TEAS 538

FLORENCE NIGHTINGALE
Bettmann Archives

Florence Nightingale

Colleen A. Hobbs

Twayne Publishers
An Imprint of Simon & Schuster Macmillan
New York

Prentice Hall International
London • Mexico City • New Delhi • Singapore • Sydney • Toronto

Twayne's English Authors Series No. 538

Florence Nightingale
Colleen A. Hobbs

Twayne Publishers
An Imprint of Simon & Schuster Macmillan
1633 Broadway
New York, NY 10019

Library of Congress Cataloging-in-Publication Data

Hobbs, Colleen Adele.
    Florence Nightingale. Colleen A. Hobbs.
        p. cm. — (Twayne's English authors series ; TEAS 538)
    Includes bibliographical references (p. 97) and index.
    ISBN 0-8057-7802-0 (alk. paper)
    1. Nightingale, Florence, 1820–1910—Criticism and interpretation.
I. Title. II. Series: Twayne's English authors series ; 538.
RT37.N5H62   1997
610.73'092—dc21   97-18783
[B]   CIP

The paper used in this publication meets the minimum requirements of American
National Standard for Information Sciences—Permanence of Paper for Printed Library
Materials. ANSI Z39.48–1984. ∞™

10 9 8 7 6 5 4 3 2

Printed in the United States of America

For Kappy

Contents

Preface

Florence Nightingale entered the public stage in the middle of the nineteenth century, an entrance made possible by the bungled military campaign and poorly administered hospitals in the Crimea. From the Crimean War emerged a Victorian ideal: the heroic military nurse who remained the compassionate, feminine caregiver. The Nightingale legend and fame grew from her 18-month service in army hospitals, but that enduring image of simple altruism does a disservice to a complex and often contradictory character.

This study has examined those complexities in Nightingale's enormous collection of correspondence, privately printed texts, and administrative writings. In recent editions of Nightingale's early letters and travel literature, readers can see the "lady with a lamp" as she painstakingly gathers health care information, rationalizes the nursing schemes that make little sense to her social peers, and constructs an independent life for herself. Nightingale's feminist essay "Cassandra" is now widely anthologized and studied; new editions of *Suggestions for Thought*, her theological tome, amplify her popular manifesto and allow it to be read in its context. And finally, Nightingale's writings on reform, most available only on microfiche, offer insight into her work as a de facto cabinet member. As she produced government reports on the health of the British soldier, Nightingale mastered the tedious administrative details that, with tenacity and determination, could lead to meaningful change in the army's hospitals. In addition, though, she wrote her personality large across her reform texts, instilling in them her outrage, her pugnacity, and her trademark exaggeration and humor.

Florence Nightingale was neither a saint nor the creator of modern nursing. She was irascible and often quick to find fault. She played political games and could be brutal to the doctors, nurses, or administrators she viewed as her opponents or competitors. Many other women nursed more patients, managed more hospitals, or more readily adopted the modern principles of contagion and infection. Yet her public acclaim linked her inextricably to the cause of nursing. Because of her social position, her government connections, and a stroke of good timing, Nightingale had access to a bully pulpit: She spent the rest of her long life trying to improve public health and to alleviate the suffering of the

British soldier. In the course of first developing her nursing vocation and then lobbying for the health of the army, Florence Nightingale the nurse increasingly became Florence Nightingale the author. In the wealth of her writing, we witness her battles with government ineptitude, sexual and social mores, and her own inner demons. Nightingale once declared that she had lived her life in a breakneck "fever." The saintly persona of popular culture pales in the presence of Nightingale's writing, texts that offer modern readers the best sense of her "neck or nothing" pace and her extraordinary life.

Acknowledgments

This exploration of Florence Nightingale was assisted by the generosity of many people. My interest in this project grew from Professor Janet Larson's work on Florence Nightingale and Victorian women's religious writings. Her encouragement and support made my own research possible. Professor Herbert Sussman provided invaluable advice on organization and revision. Gabriella Gandara assisted with the painstaking work of tracking permissions. Jennifer Farthing at Twayne Publishers tracked the manuscript through the editing and production process. Ken Mayer and Liz Smith took time away from their own projects to answer questions on Roman antiquities. My warmest thanks to all. And to David Woodruff, for his patience and stoicism, my best love.

Chronology

1859   Begins work with the Royal Commission on the Sanitary State of the Army in India.

1860   Publishes *Notes on Nursing: What It Is, and What It Is Not.* Revised version of *Suggestions for Thought* privately printed. Nightingale School of Nursing begins operation.

1863   Publishes *Observations on Evidence Contained in the Stational Reports Submitted to Her by the Royal Commission on the Sanitary State of the Army in India;* and *Notes on Hospitals.*

1871   Publishes *Introductory Notes on Lying-in Institutions: Together with a Proposal for Organising an Institution for Training Midwives and Midwifery Nurses.*

1907   Receives Order of Merit from King Edward VII.

1910   Florence Nightingale dies 13 August.

Chapter One
Nightingale as Author

Florence Nightingale's historical reputation is a paradoxical one: although her name is widely recognized, few people are certain of exactly what she did to become so famous. The strong-minded, often difficult government administrator would be mortified—or perhaps merely amused—to know that her hagiographic biographers have portrayed her as primarily a *nurse,* and a rather saintly, insipid one at that. Nursing, she declared, was "the least important of all the functions into which she had been forced."[1] For 18 months during an otherwise forgettable war, Nightingale supervised a group of nurses in a British military hospital. She procured food and clothing for an army that was left starving and naked by bureaucratic ineptitude.

Nightingale's service from 1854 to 1855 offered the British public a model of competence and heroism that was sorely lacking in the military. The British army's miserable performance in the Crimean War was notable for—but not limited to—the disastrous slaughter of the Light Brigade. Nightingale's heroism, too, was of exactly the right sort, neither overtly threatening to government authority nor dangerously masculine. In the Florence Nightingale mythology, the stalwart British soldier was served by the feminine ideal: "[T]he woman was hard-working and gentle; furthermore, she reached a final fulfillment and happiness in a life of service, offering herself wholly to care for the male."[2] With the backing of enormous public goodwill, Nightingale helped create a new paradigm for nurses, one that transformed the capable, working-class domiciliary nurse and midwife into a modern nurse whose work was defined by selflessness, morality, and training that legitimized the profession for women of status and privilege.[3] For the Victorian public, the Florence Nightingale story was one in which women helped men become heroes.

A contemporary song in which Nightingale "prays for the dying, she gives peace to the brave," is typical in its depiction of her as a rarefied angel.[4] Despite this portrayal as the soldiers' nurturing savior, Nightingale's most lasting contributions to the British army developed from her postwar years of unromantic administrative reform. In Henry Wads-

1

worth Longfellow's famous poem "Santa Filomena," soldiers kiss the
shadow of "A Lady with a Lamp." Yet the Saint Florence who battled to
improve conditions in military hospitals raged sarcastically at the War
Office that "deserves the V.C. [Victoria Cross] for cool intrepidity in the
face of facts."[5] Even less saintly is her exultation in a hard-won bureaucratic victory: When her skillful political maneuvering carried the day,
she gloated that "I defeated them by a trick they were too stupid to find
out" (Life, 2:7). In candid correspondence, Oxford don Benjamin Jowett
repeatedly scolds her about her temper. The master of Balliol College
takes her to task for swearing, as well as for her intemperate criticism of
opponents in hospital reform. "My hatreds are so mean compared with
yours," he says, analyzing her response to "public enemies"; referring to
one of his translations from Greek, he recalls, "I think that you once said
D—— Thucydides."[6] In matters of sanitation reform, Nightingale's
focus was single-minded and her wrath, scathing. From the Crimea, she
makes no apology for her scorn of official incompetence, observing to an
ally, "If you have friends among these men [doctors she criticizes], so
have I. But I would have given up my own father in such a cause."[7]

Nightingale's heroic but simplistic reputation as a saintly nurse grew
from her own popularity, the result of her representation in innumerable
ballads, portraits, and Staffordshire figurines. The reputation was maintained, in part, by Nightingale's own duplicity. She effectively concealed
her long administrative career by refusing credit for much of her work.
Nightingale believed that a woman could achieve administrative reform
only if her influence remained a secret, and she worked in calculated
anonymity. A letter regarding reforms in India is typical: She urges the
governor of Bombay to appoint an ally as surgeon general but asks "the
great favor that if Lord Reay thinks well to exert his power in this matter, he will do it entirely from himself, & not mention my name at all."[8]

Nightingale often sought to keep a low profile, but her literary reputation assured her fame in the twentieth century. Scholars have canonized
Nightingale's essay "Cassandra" in the tradition of classic feminist tracts
such as Mary Wollstonecraft's A Vindication of the Rights of Woman. "Cassandra" was written while Nightingale was rejecting the expectations of
her privileged social class and battling her family's disapproval. The text
takes the name of the unheeded Greek prophetess to argue against the
waste of women's time and talents. Nightingale rages against the idleness
and boredom of the Victorian drawing room, asking, "Why have women
passion, intellect, moral activity—these three—and a place in society
where no one of these three can be exercised?"[9] A thinly veiled, emotional

autobiography, "Cassandra" paints a devastating picture of the leisured class's treatment of its daughters. John Stuart Mill was struck by Nightingale's perspective on her social circle and praised "the exhibition it contains of what life is in this country among the classes in easy circumstances, being earnestly and feelingly and many parts forcibly done, and so evidently the result of personal observation."[10] From her position as an insider, Nightingale passionately depicts the desperation of intelligent women who are confined by custom and circumstance, illustrating her argument with pointed details about the sham of "successful" social marriages and pomposity of formal dinners, which she ridicules as the "great sacrament" of the day (*Cassandra,* 210).

"Cassandra" is Nightingale's best-known text, but its depiction of her feminism is somewhat misleading. After her return from the Crimea, Nightingale concerned herself with exacting change from an existing administrative system rather than working to change the system itself. She had little patience with the agitation of women authors she called "female ink-bottles," and forgetting the advantages of her own wealth and social status, she convinced herself that women were hampered only by their aversion to hard work. In correspondence with journalist Harriet Martineau in 1861, Nightingale declared that she was "brutally indifferent to the wrongs or rights of my sex" (*Life,* 1:385). The perspective represented in "Cassandra" does not represent Nightingale's final word on the subject of women's rights; to appreciate her contradictions, readers must balance this brief essay with Nightingale's later thoughts on the subject.

Until recently, access to Nightingale's diverse, widely scattered body of writing has been difficult to obtain. Some of her texts, such as *Letters from Egypt* or *Suggestions for Thought,* were privately printed, with only a limited number of copies produced. Her arguments for reform often appear anonymously, hidden under the names of obscure government commissions. After illness confined Nightingale to bed in 1857, she conducted most of her business through the mail. The result is a trove of almost 15,000 letters—most of which remain uncollected. A happy exception is Martha Vicinus and Bea Nergaard's edition of Nightingale's letters, which illustrates the enormous range of her correspondence.[11] Other collections of letters focus on specific biographical experiences: Nightingale's travels, her wartime service, and her association with Benjamin Jowett.[12]

Many of the works that were available only in research libraries or literary archives are now more accessible, thanks to increased scholarly attention to this complex historical and literary figure. Interest in "Cassandra" has resulted in two different editions of *Suggestions for Thought,* one that focuses on Nightingale's examination of religious and philosophical ideas and another that looks more closely at the text's feminist debate.[13] In addition, microfiche copies of many of Nightingale's official government reports are now available through the efforts of the Adelaide Nutting historical nursing archive.[14]

From these new editions of her work, a picture of Florence Nightingale, author, has begun to emerge. In her own writing, the imposing, monolithic Victorian heroine gives way to a contradictory and thoroughly entertaining nineteenth-century woman. Nightingale's trademark satire—her impatience for reform combined with her dry humor—is manifest throughout her work. Complaining of governmental indecision, for example, she declares that "I do not know if Hamlet was mad but he would have driven me mad" (*Miss Nightingale Said,* 35). Her own poor health becomes the subject of ridicule: She calls her inexplicable illness "Thorn in the Flesh," or "T in F" for short (103). Referring to her mother's family, Nightingale once said that "[w]e Smiths all exaggerate" (*Life,* 2:238). As she conducts the difficult, politically charged work of reform, that bent toward exaggeration manifests itself in histrionic, self-pitying, and completely human complaints. For example, she is not above comparing her suffering to Christ's and bewailing her own martyrdom. "Christ was betrayed by one," she writes to her aunt Mai, "but my cause has been betrayed by everyone—ruined, betrayed, destroyed by everyone alas" (*Duty,* 165).

In her grim recitation of incidents in military hospitals, though, even satire fails her. As she remembers the lost Crimean soldiers, Nightingale is neither martyr, nor saint, nor heroine. She is simply heartbroken when, in a private note of 1856, she writes, "I stand at the altar of the murdered men, and while I live, I fight their cause" (*Life,* 1:318). The compassion and contradictions of this utterly fallible public figure are a reflection of the political battlefield on which she played. Nightingale conducted a reform campaign through savvy, ambition, and sheer force of will, using methods that were pragmatic, expedient, and sometimes gleefully underhanded. Her numerous texts on travel, religion, sanitation, and politics clearly illustrate that her tactics were not ideologically consistent. Her writing proves, also, that in her passion and persistence, she was true to her "murdered men."

Chapter Two

Nightingale's Early Life and Travels

Florence Nightingale's privileged upbringing seems unlikely to have fostered an interest in the unfeminine tasks of hospital nursing and administration. Her father, William Shore Nightingale (called W. E. N.), had inherited a fortune at a young age and consequently, his daughter observed, "has never known what struggle is" (*Ever Yours*, 46). Her mother, the lovely Frances (Fanny) Smith, had a gift for lavish entertaining and, Nightingale declared, had "obtained by her own exertions, the best society in England." Her family divided the year between London, during the social season, and two country houses. In later years, Nightingale's friend Benjamin Jowett teased her that when she returned from the Crimea, "you might have become a Duchess if you had played your cards better" (*Jowett's Letters*, 280). Marriage to a duke might have been a surprise but not unheard of in the Nightingale family. Nightingale's older sister, Parthenope, eventually married the wealthy Sir Harry Verney and became mistress of Claydon House, the historic Verney family home. Nightingale's onetime fiancé, Richard Monckton Milnes, was later made the first Baron Houghton.

At her mother's insistence, Nightingale's family became respectable Anglicans, but her background included a Unitarian streak that emphasized humanism and an interest in progressive social causes such as abolition and labor reform. Perhaps because of his Unitarian background, Nightingale's father insisted on tutoring his two daughters himself. Parthenope ("Parthe" to her family) showed less interest in her father's Greek and Latin lessons than in her mother's social obligations. His younger daughter, however, became his avid pupil. Florence studied history, philosophy, and modern languages such as French, German, and Italian. She even asked for additional schooling in mathematics, which she received over her mother's objections.

Nightingale's education was an outward manifestation of a separation from her mother and sister's domestic, feminine realm. She was dissatisfied with the social duties demanded of her and was increasingly aware that her family's hopes for her future—a brilliant marriage, a lovely family, spectacular parties—were much different than her own. She complained that "a country-house is the real place for dissipation. Sometimes I think that everybody is hard upon me, that to be for ever expected to be looking merry and saying something lively is more than can be asked mornings, noons, and nights" (*Life,* 1:40). When her mother set her to work counting the linens and china, she was acutely self-conscious of the house's expensive appointments. "Can reasonable people want all this?" she asked her friend Mary Clarke Mohl in 1847. "Is it even good Political Economy . . . to invent wants in order to supply employment?" (1:42). Nightingale's resistance to the life her family enjoyed increasingly strained domestic relations; a letter from Elizabeth Gaskell reports Fanny's tearful confession that the Nightingales "are ducks, and have hatched a wild swan" (1:139).

Nightingale's rejection of her class's expectations grew in part from a strong religious commitment. A few months before her 17th birthday, she recorded that "[o]n February 7th, 1837, God spoke to me and called me into His service."[1] The form of that service was not revealed to her, but a nursing vocation gradually began to take shape. She stated that "since I was twenty-four [in 1844], there never was any vagueness in my plans or ideas as to what God's work was for me" (*Florence,* 33). With this clarity of vision, she began her practical study, a comprehensive survey of modern nursing that was remarkable for a woman of her youth and privileged social class. While she conferred with public health experts and gathered materials on sanitation and mortality statistics, she was effectively preparing for her role in the Crimean War in 1854, creating for herself a course of study otherwise unavailable. Quietly and privately, she acted on a spiritual vocation, a religious calling that justified her unorthodox decision and allowed her to remain committed to a mission despite discouragement.

Nightingale's call to modernize nursing was especially complicated by her family's united, unwavering disapproval. The Nightingales' horror at their brilliant daughter's interest in hospitals reflected nineteenth-century social realities. Florence was a charming, talented young woman with an enviable reputation in society; her mother harbored hopes of a match with either Florence's cousin Henry Nicholson or the philanthropist Monckton Milnes. Issues of class and status made the choice of hospital work seem particularly inappropriate and unacceptable. In an age when all but the indigent were cared for in their own homes, hospitals had earned reputations for filth and immorality. Sarah Gamp, the

Martin Chuzzlewit nurse who requires her half-pint of porter to be "brought reg'lar and draw'd mild," is Charles Dickens's 1843 depiction of the slatternly professional stereotype.[2] In 1854, Nightingale recorded a head nurse's observation that "in the course of her large experience she had never known a nurse who was not drunken, and there was immoral conduct practised in the very wards" (*Florence*, 41). Unmarried, unchaperoned nurses shared wards with doctors, leading Nightingale to wonder how a successful nurse "disposed of the difficulties of surgeons making love to her, and of living with the women of indifferent character who generally make the nurses of hospitals" (*Life*, 1:63). Women of Florence Nightingale's social prominence did not conduct charity work in public hospitals, and her mother and sister were scandalized by implications of such conduct. "It was as if I had wanted to be a kitchen-maid," she said later (1:60).

An incident from December 1845 illustrates the ongoing tension that the issue of hospital work created in the Nightingale family. Florence proposed to undertake training at the nearby Salisbury Infirmary, an institution headed by Dr. Richard Fowler, an old family friend. Mrs. Fowler subsequently deemed the project inappropriate, and Parthenope greeted the suggestion with reproaches and hysterics. Fanny saw the event as an occasion for an illicit romance, accusing her daughter of "an attachment of which she was ashamed [with a] low vulgar surgeon" (*Florence*, 38). With her plan wrecked and her family incensed, Nightingale recalled that "my misery and vacuity afterwards were indescribable" (*Life*, 1:59). In her diary, she recorded bitter, inconsolable disappointment: "God has something for me to do for him—or he would have let me die some time ago. . . . This morning I felt as if my soul would pass away in tears—in utter loneliness—in a bitter passion of tears & agony of solitude but I live. . . . Oh for some great thing to sweep this loathsome life into the past" (*Ever Yours*, 28–29). Such domestic conflicts were enacted repeatedly, causing Nightingale to observe in her diary that "there are Private Martyrs as well as burnt or drowned ones" (*Life*, 1:59). The constant conflict exhausted the entire household; in the fall of 1847, Nightingale collapsed after months of inadequate food and sleep. As the forbidding London social season loomed before her, she confessed to her friend Mary Clarke Mohl that "the prospect of three winter months of perpetual row" was more than she could bear (*Florence*, 46). In the hope that their daughter's obsession would be forgotten in the excitement of travel, the Nightingales agreed to send her to Rome for the winter. To offer the entire family a respite, then, Florence took a Roman holiday that lasted from October 1847 until April 1848. Nightingale's sister, showing the effects of prolonged family feuding, gave thanks for Florence's opportunity to travel: "God is very good to provide such a pleasant time" (*Life*, 1:69–70).

The trip was arranged by Charles and Selina Bracebridge, a couple that Nightingale later called "the creators of my life" (*Life*, 2:236). Mohl introduced the families in 1846, and the wealthy, childless Bracebridges treated Florence's ambition for hospital work as a legitimate endeavor. Being taken seriously "changes the aspect of things to one," Nightingale wrote to Selina Bracebridge, declaring that "since I have known you I have shaken hands with life."[3] As the trip was planned, Parthe expressed genuine hope that her sister's companion had "the taste and the affection which will most give her [Florence] happiness" (*Life*, 1:69). The older woman, whom Florence affectionately nicknamed "Σ," or Sigma, provided support that proved critical to her charge's emotional health and to the development of her nursing agenda. "She never told me life was fair and my share of its blessings great and that I ought to be happy. She did not know that I was miserable but she felt it," Nightingale said. "She had the heart and the instinct to say—'Earth, my child, has a grave and in heaven there is rest' " (*Florence*, 46). The bond between the two was so great that Nightingale took to recording her thoughts in the form of a dialogue with "Σ," of whom she said, "There is a woman in whom to trust" (*Study*, 116). The influential Bracebridges of Atherston Hall fully satisfied the Nightingales' requirements for social respectability, and their intervention on behalf of 27-year-old Florence provided her with an interlude of unprecedented freedom. Nightingale claimed that "I never enjoyed any time in my life so much as my time at Rome" (*Life*, 1:79).

The numerous letters that Nightingale sent from Rome, and subsequently from Egypt, are important if only for their historical record and their literary merit. Nightingale's letters home illustrate the conventions of Victorian travel and, in the process, reveal the ideology of a nineteenth-century British tourist confronting the Catholic South and the infidel East. The letters' timing, however, makes them particularly useful for understanding nineteenth-century history and Nightingale's own development. Her letters from Rome coincide with the failed Italian revolution of 1848, the period of "Risorgimento," or resurrection. The uprising that Nightingale witnessed and supported ultimately was quelled, but the impulse would end with Italian nationalists expelling French and Austrian powers to form their own state. Her letters from the Nile show the West's fascination with the land of the pharaohs and the practice of Victorian Egyptology. Most important, the letters offer an opportunity to examine the young woman who is not yet a national heroine. Before she tackles the overwhelming problems of health care in the British army and becomes the "Santa Filomena" of Longfellow's poem, Nightingale's holiday letters describe her exploration of art, history, and politics, revealing the engaging personality that charmed her social circle. Her vivid, detailed travelogue and wry humor show a lighter side of a character famous for her compassion and tireless humanitarian efforts. In addition, though, her letters record the despair that ultimately allowed her to break with her family and to begin her life's work.

"Some to Be Amused, and Some Come to Be Shocked": Nightingale's Roman Holiday

Nightingale's holiday chronicles begin on 28 October 1847, the day after she crossed the Channel to Le Havre, France. Her descriptions of midcentury land, rail, and ship travel indicate high spirits and a keen sense of fun. For example, a French boat delayed by fog provided an occasion for people-watching. She and Selina Bracebridge left the company of English women in the "ladies' cabin" to join a crush of people "talking Arabic, French, Irish, everything but English." There, she observed, "we could not well be in any place more amusing" (*Nightingale in Rome,* 15). She drew pictures of French railway stations; she noted the French porter's tattoo of the crucifixion, complete with Napoleon standing under the cross. During the rough overland trip to Marseille, she told her family that she took consolation in the fact that "none of you (unless you have been in America) were ever on such a road, in such a vehicle. . . . I kept my eyelids and lips *tight* shut, lest my eyes and teeth should jump out, and I not be able to find them in the dark" (35). The lure of Rome transcended inconveniences and boorish travelers, and as the boat from Genoa approached the Eternal City, Nightingale became strangely serious. Anticipating the sight of St. Peter's church, she spent "the most solemn night of my life" in preparation. Alone on the boat deck near the island of Elba, she saw "a little white mist . . . which took the shape of the figure (and the light of the glory round the head) of our Saviour when he walked upon the sea. . . . I wondered whether any of us would have had faith enough like Peter [k]new, to risk to sink" (41). Nightingale's Rome is the city of St. Peter's, the center of Christendom that is a little closer to heaven than England and the family home at Embley. Just the thought of the holy city steadies her faith as she, like the biblical St. Peter, faces intimidating "risks." Nightingale's vision of Christ, seen on the eve of her arrival, indicates Rome's compelling inspiration.

For most Victorian tourists, Rome was a virtual winter playground, a city of Carnival and carriage parades down the Corso. Before Italian unification, northern Europeans viewed the Papal States as a site of picturesque revelry, "divided and 'backward,' the home of emotion and superstition (Catholicism with pagan shadowings) rather than enlightenment."[4] As early as 1820, Charlotte Eaton described a group of sightseers clambering to the top of St. Peter's, hoisting themselves onto the horizontal bar of the cross, and singing "God Save the King."[5] John Murray's 1843 *Handbook for Travellers in Central Italy* helped simplify the travails of travel, providing British tourists with reliable references for accommodations and historic sites. By 1856, William Makepeace Thackeray remarked on the insular habits of English travelers. The protagonist of *The Newcomes* observes that "our friend is an Englishman, and did at Rome as the English do."[6] Nightingale herself mocked tourists' philistine attitudes when she described Mr. Bracebridge's somewhat unsophisticated relatives: "Some people, my dear parents, come to Rome to spend the winter, some people to study the Arts, some to learn the antiquities, some to be amused, and some come to be shocked. . . . They [the relatives] have been shocked at St. Peter's, they have been shocked at St. John in Lateran, they have been shocked in their own apartments. . . . As they have come to Rome for this purpose, I might if I had been in a benevolent frame of mind, have furthered their object by propounding some extraordinary doctrines, but I wasn't" (*Nightingale in Rome*, 147).

When annoyed, Nightingale could dismiss English sightseers as "the plagues of Egypt," but she herself arrived with her father's detailed list of attractions and a generous supply of guidebooks (*Nightingale in Rome*, 254). In answer to her family's questions, she dutifully reports her sightseeing activities: She describes her visits to the catacombs, her impressions of the frescos in Raphael's Loggia, and the day spent at the Forum with a map and a tourist guide. Like Thackeray's fictional character, she participated in the British community's activities in Rome, attending the usual rounds of dinners, balls, and teas. She was charmed by Sidney and Elizabeth Herbert, friends of the Bracebridges who introduced her to a circle of acquaintances that included Dr. Henry Manning, the future cardinal. Even in the Herberts' pleasant company, Nightingale resisted time-consuming social obligations, finding that "I have often regretted our solitude, and never have enjoyed anything half so much, nor entered into it half so deeply as my solitary excursions" (97). Celebrated figures failed to impress her, and her description of American essayist Margaret Fuller is brief and unflattering: "[S]he does drawl out Transcendentalism in such a voice" (78). Her patience with etiquette also could be short. After describing the complications of accepting a family's invitation to tea, she despaired at all possibilities and decided merely to avoid the family in question: "In the next world I hope we shall meet—in this it is impossible" (200).

She faithfully described villas, museums, and fountains as she checked them off her father's list, but Rome's importance in Nightingale's spiritual life ensured that her letters revealed as much about her religious sensibilities as about sightseeing tours. St. Peter's remained her touchstone. She returned there to attend masses and political rallies, to view its works of art, and to conduct her own silent meditations. On her first morning in Rome, she left her bed before dawn to race alone to the church. Her letter home declared that "no event in my life, except my death can ever be greater than that first entrance into St. Peter's, the concentrated spirit of the Christianity of so many years. . . . [I]t was not an artistic effect it made on me—it was the effect of the presence of God" (*Nightingale in Rome,* 28). All other houses of worship fade in comparison: the Established Church of England outside the city walls is a mere "Communion of Bonnets" where she "had great difficulty in seeing Him in the midst of us" (43). Nightingale was baptized Anglican, and her family came from a dissenting Unitarian background, but her visits to St. Peter's were so frequent that she felt compelled to assure her family that she would not convert to Catholicism. As the next chapter will discuss, Nightingale's religious beliefs were eclectic and often heterodox; she was drawn not to Catholic doctrine but to St. Peter's serenity, its ability to provide her with a haven and a center for her private worship. Despite the comfort of St. Peter's, she contends that Catholicism had nothing for her "to lay hold of" (155).

The Catholic institution that most nearly offered Nightingale a "hold" was the convent. As early as 1843, an exasperated Fanny wrote to W. E. N., "perhaps if we got a Soeur de Charité Flo would let us rest in some peace" (*Florence,* 32). Sisters of Charity were a popular topic for mid-century Britons because the Oxford Movement had revived holy orders for Anglican women. Eventually, even dissenting Protestant branches estab-

lished such women's institutions, which often operated schools, orphan-
ages, and—most important to Nightingale—hospitals.[7] Before Nightingale helped improve the reputation of nursing, convents or "sisterhoods"
were the only place in Victorian society where women's hospital training
was accepted and encouraged. Here, in both Catholic and Protestant facilities, nurses could escape the "Sarah Gamp" stereotype. Nightingale held
the Catholic Church in high regard for valuing women's contributions and
for providing them with meaningful work. At one point, she even considered founding a Protestant order of her own.

Nightingale visited hospitals whenever she traveled, and Rome was
no exception. By January 1848, her survey was well under way, and she
reported, "I have been doing a course of convents and hospitals"
(*Nightingale in Rome*, 175). A Protestant woman's access to Roman
Catholic hospitals was not always assured, and in one instance, Nightingale's determination was tested. In January 1848, she victoriously
reported bullying a monsignor to enter the Hospital of S. Spirito, a large
general hospital near the Vatican that also provided care for foundlings.
With Mrs. Bracebridge and the influential Elizabeth Herbert by her
side, Nightingale stretched the truth to carry the day: "[T]he hospital,
he said, couldn't be opened at all hours, it was not to be expected. . . . In
a half scolding, half complaining voice, he asked whether we were going
to leave Rome soon. Nobody answered, so I thought they meant me to
tell the lie, and bowing to the earth, I replied *very* soon [the party left
three months later]. Well then, he said, when do you want to see the
Convent? Tomorrow, I said. It's too soon, he said, we can't get it ready.
Well then Wednesday, I said very angrily. And do you want to see the
Conservatorio *too*, in a despairing tone. To be sure, I said" (174–75).
Nightingale reports that Mrs. Herbert made the group's apologies to
the monsignor because "I was laughing too much." Unrepentantly, she
observes that her behavior "was so truly impudent—Inglesissimo, is the
only adjective it deserves. However we got what we wanted."

Nightingale's tours of Roman hospitals required no other displays of
impudence, and she viewed facilities with a practiced, professional eye.
After the fight for entrance to S. Spirito, she dismisses the hospital as "a
hopeless case" (*Nightingale in Rome*, 195). In contrast, the French sisters
of the Conservatorio win her praise: they were "so different from the
grubby nuns I have seen in other places" (194). Her letters noted the
inefficient organization of hospital wards, the dangers of overcrowding,
and the lack of ventilation and exercise for patients. In particular, a facility for "scrofulous children" has "no gardens, no place for air or exercise

or anything to cure [them]" (190). At S. Giacomo, a hospital for incurable diseases, "the stench [is] dreadful, the locale cold, airless, dark—the nuns perfectly over done,—it seemed a physical impossibility for any one ever to get well there" (190). These visits confirmed her conviction of the importance of proper drainage, sewage disposal, and general sanitation.

Nightingale fumed at hospital conditions in Rome and imagined that her beloved pope could institute reforms. "I wish I could write Pio Nono a note to come here. They do not even wash with hot water," she wrote disparagingly of the hospital S. Gallicano (*Nightingale in Rome,* 191). But hospital conditions were universally poor, and the administrative abuses of the Scutari hospitals are foreshadowed eerily in a description of Pius IX's unannounced visit to S. Spirito. There, the pope encountered the same uncooperative monsignor visited by Nightingale's party. The church contributed generously to the hospital, but as Pius angrily discovered, fraud and incompetent management left patients in filthy conditions with inedible food and insufficient medicine. In the Crimea, Nightingale would rage against the bureaucratic bungling that cost the lives of thousands of British soldiers; in 1848, her letters described the pope flinging a bowl of soup to the ground, crying, "[T]his filth for my poor people!" (183). Her experience in Rome showed Nightingale that sound hospital administration eluded even the exalted head of the Holy Catholic Church.

If the Nightingales believed that a Roman vacation would cure their daughter's interest in hospitals, they were mistaken. Away from the disapproval of her family and the confines of British society, her work continued to take shape, and her spiritual life—the belief that God had chosen her for his work—only deepened. She brought her nursing agenda with her to Rome, and she furthered her mission with study and empirical analysis. The trip was propitious in yet another regard. The charming Sidney Herbert, whose wife Elizabeth negotiated entrance into S. Spirito's hospital, would serve as secretary for war during the Crimean conflict. On her Roman holiday, Nightingale met Herbert, the man who would make possible her mission to Turkey, the man who would become her tireless partner in hospital and sanitation reform. Nightingale's excursion was very much a working vacation, one that expanded the knowledge and contacts her calling required. A description of the Ludovisi Juno, a statue she calls "the Goddess of Liberty," indicates that the freedoms allowed Nightingale in Rome contrasted sharply with her memories of home. For her, the image of the goddess captured the essence of freedom, and "no one who has not known and sadly felt the want of freedom in *word* and *action* can tell how to value enough the freedom of *thought* as a privilege for oneself, and to respect it in others, and to love it till it becomes a personal presence—that is why I do so adore this Juno" (*Nightingale in Rome*, 220).

As she struggled to gain her family's acceptance of her nursing agenda, Nightingale imagined herself fighting a battle for "freedom in *word* and *action*." On a grand scale, this was the battle being waged in Italy, where revolutionaries were fighting to throw off foreign rule. Nightingale enthusiastically supported their efforts, and her letters closely followed the events of "the Quarantotto," or "the 48," a year in which the kingdoms of the Italian peninsula faced revolts or agitation for more democratic forms of government. In this year of singular changes, citizens of the fragmented states controlled by Austria and France grew to think of themselves not only as Romans, Lombards, or Sicilians but also as Italians united in struggle. In Rome, Pius IX had quickly earned a reputation as a reforming pope, declaring amnesty for political prisoners soon after his election in 1847. Shortly after reaching Rome in November, Nightingale reported on the pope with unbounded patriotic idealism: "Here one has been longing and praying for Italian regeneration ever since one can remember anything, but always looking for it in the way of the re-establishment of the Italian republics, and one would as soon have thought of expecting it from a Pope, from the church, as from an old nurse—and here it has come from the very centre of corruption and conservation itself. . . . Pius looks like the man to carry it out" (*Nightingale in Rome,* 34). Well aware that she was witnessing historic changes, she described in detail the pope's reinstitution of municipal government. As she listed the composition of the Roman assembly and council in mid-November, she declared that "it is a day taken from out of heaven and put down upon earth, a day apart from the rest of one's life, an epic poem condensed into one hour of common existence" (47).

Events of the Quarantotto unfolded with Nightingale's unbounded support for the apparently liberal government of Pius, part of the "cult of Pio Nono" that historian G. M. Trevelyan says "was for some months the religion of Italy, and of Liberals and exiles all over the world."[8] Like the Italian nationalists, Nightingale put too much stock in Pius's endorsement of administrative change; as the struggle intensified, he opposed Italian unification and maintained control only with the support of Napoleon III's troops. Nightingale's family was skeptical of

Pius's intentions, but their daughter countered their reservations with sound scolding. In January 1848 she wrote, "My dearest people, I am really ashamed of you. Don't speak to me in that manner. I am surrounded here by enemies of Pius, and shall I find foes in mine own household?" (*Nightingale in Rome*, 166). Because of Pius's relaxation of censorship, she was able to read political newspapers and relay to her family the latest revelations of scandal and corruption. Explaining the pope's innumerable orders and administrative changes, Nightingale evaded criticism of her fixation on papal reforms by reminding her family who had schooled her in politics: "I can never be sufficiently thankful to Papa for having given me an interest in Statistical and Political Matters" (72).

The revolution in Rome was exhilarating, and Nightingale records her participation, celebrating when the municipal assembly marched to St. Peter's and cheering when the Italian flag was raised at the Capitol. "I was certainly born to be a tag-rag-and-bob-tail," she writes to her cousin Hilary Bonham Carter, "for when I hear of a popular demonstration, I am nothing better than a ragamuffin" (*Study*, 138). A letter written in the midst of the Sicilian uprising against Neapolitan rule is dated, "Rome, this glorious day of her liberty. January 21, 1848" (*Nightingale in Rome*, 181). By March, the revolution had spread to Milan, where "The Glorious Five Days" of civilian street fighting ended in the defeat of the Austrian army. Describing the Milanese citizens' defense of their city, she exclaimed, "If 1848 sees the foreigner out of Italy, what an age to live in! I think the kingdom of God is coming" (281). A year later, France and Austria successfully quelled rebel uprisings and proved that the "kingdom of God" was not yet at hand. Even at that distance, Nightingale retained her revolutionary fervor. She observed that the Italians' defeat would not be final because the revolution had "raised the Romans in the moral scale, and in their own esteem." She was particularly indignant at critics who accused Italian nationalists of "vandalism" for exposing their historic monuments to damage: "I should like to see them fight the streets inch by inch, till the last man dies at his barricade, till St. Peter's is level with the ground, till the Vatican is blown into the air. . . . [T]hen, and not till then, would Europe do justice to France as a thief and a murderer. . . . If I were in Rome, I should be the first to fire the Sistine, turning my head aside, and Michael Angelo would cry, 'Well done,' as he saw his work destroyed" (*Study*, 151–52). The "glorious" uprising in Milan, which Nightingale saw as the blossoming of secular and religious liberty, brought an end to her Italian travels. Rome's own

political stability was now in question. On Lady Day, Nightingale told
her family that although she would "like to pull a trigger against the
Austrian," they should "admire our prudence and trust in our cow-
ardice" (*Nightingale in Rome*, 284). She was coming home, but she continued to follow politics passionately. Retreating from the city, she read
the new Roman constitution by opening a stranger's mail, although the
postmaster "only allowed [us] to commit larceny for ten minutes" (275).

Many of Nightingale's aspirations had borne fruit in Rome. A religious retreat at the Convent of the Trinitá dei Monti further confirmed
her belief in her nursing vocation. She was befriended there by the sympathetic Madre Santa Colomba, a woman who became her spiritual
guide and received "divine messages" concerning Nightingale's mission.
Nightingale recorded an exchange between the two in which the madre
asked, "Did not God speak to you during this retreat?" Nightingale
replied, "He asked me to surrender my will . . . [t]o all that is upon the
earth" (*Study*, 144–145). Nightingale's religious retreat validated her
belief that God had a mission for her, and she resolved anew to put her
calling into action. The madre's heavenly messages told her to "turn
her whole heart to God that she might be ready to do his work" (144). This
spiritual resolution was aided by the practical benefits of making further
hospital inspections and useful connections. Most important, perhaps,
her experience of the Quarantotto allowed her to share in a momentary
triumph of human spirit. In Rome, Nightingale witnessed insurrection,
political change, and the blossoming of hope. The city for her was more
than just the sanctuary of her beautiful St. Peter's, the church she could
imagine "level with the ground." It had come to stand for a kind of spiritual perfection, a moment in which, free of distraction and social con-
straints, she could picture the impossible. St. Peter's faith was tested
when Christ asked him to walk on water; Nightingale believed that hers
was tested when God called her to "surrender" herself to hospital service. In the midst of Italy's revolution, Nightingale could envision
miraculous changes. She wanted to savor that moment: "I should like to
keep my vision of Rome as a purely distinct and undivided recollection
of my life, a jewel for which no setting is wanted, for which no setting is
sufficiently valuable. Rome alone, isolated, lifted up, like a queen whom
no meaner thing is permitted to approach, an island in the sea, is how I
should like to keep her" (*Nightingale in Rome*, 276–77).

Ironically, the tourists escaping the upheaval of the Risorgimento
hurried home through France at the birth of the Second Republic. King
Louis-Philippe had been overthrown in February; arriving at Avignon in

March, the party was greeted by a Tree of Liberty. In Paris, Nightingale walked in empty streets, describing curiously *"elegant"* barricades. Her reports from Paris are stark, detailing the murders of unarmed citizens by government troops and the chaos surrounding the provisional government's attempts to restore order. Nightingale recorded the atrocities committed by both sides during the uprising, but the violence never shook her commitment to revolutionary ideals: "How can one look at the Revolution with anything but sympathy? . . . [I]f this attempt, after all others have failed, to govern itself, can carry off and employ its extra energy, how can one wish it anything but God speed, how can one but watch it with anxious hope?" (*Nightingale in Rome*, 294–95). Nightingale supported Europe's revolutions, but Paris was not, after all, her beloved Rome. Her analysis of the French revolt is tempered by her English skepticism of all things Gallic: "How can one judge for such a nation as this. . . . [W]as it possible to teach a Bourbon?"

Nightingale returned from France without incident, but England and Embley seemed dismally complacent after the excitement and intrigue of European insurrections. She was, after all, returning to the same frustrating family dynamics that had initiated her trip six months before. Although she had resolved in Rome to begin her great work, her family still expected her to meet her social obligations. By July, she had returned to the usual schedule, despairing to Mohl that "in London there have been the usual amount of Charity Balls, Charity Concerts, Charity Bazaars, whereby people bamboozle their consciences and shut their eyes. Nevertheless there does not seem the slightest prospect of a revolution here" (*Life*, 1:80). Although Nightingale's notebooks continued to chart Italian, French, and German politics after her return home (*Study*, 149), the revolution she most anticipated was a personal and domestic one. As the social status quo was confirmed, the plans she made in Rome grew dimmer, and her spirits sank.

Two events, one professional and the other personal, further complicated her return home. The family had scheduled a fall trip to Germany for Parthe's health, and Nightingale envisioned this visit as an opportunity for hospital training at the Kaiserswerth Institution, a Protestant nursing facility she had learned of in 1846. The Nightingales had objected to their daughter's attending the Salisbury Infirmary, but Kaiserswerth's religious environment made its training program above reproach. When October riots in Frankfort scuttled the trip, Nightingale mourned the lost opportunity with "cursings and swearings which relieved my disappointed feelings" (*Life*, 1:82).

Even more serious was Monckton Milnes's ultimatum. He had proposed marriage to her nine years before; now, he insisted on an answer. She reasoned that she would not be satisfied "by spending a life with him in making society and arranging domestic things"; nevertheless, accepting an unknown destiny and refusing "the man I adored" were wrenching (*Florence*, 51). Years later, after his own marriage to the Honorable Annabel Crewe, Milnes reflected on the importance of Nightingale's refusal. Visiting the Nightingale home at Lea Hurst in 1862, he writes, "This is Mr. Nightingale's house in Derbyshire in which, fourteen years ago I asked Florence Nightingale to marry me: if she had done so there would have been a heroine the less in the world & certainly not a hero the more."[9]

In the autumn of 1849, abandoning the prospect of marriage did not seem noble or heroic; it was only deeply troubling. Nightingale's mental and physical health were again precarious, and the high spirits of her Roman vacation were only a memory. She wrote to her cousin Hilary Bonham Carter that "as Rome had done her some good the family were going to send her farther afield in the hopes that that would be even better" (*Florence*, 52). The Bracebridges kindly intervened once more, and this time, the distraction was Egypt.

"This Horrid Country": Nightingale in Egypt

Europe's interest in ancient Egypt had been renewed by Napoleon's failed campaign of 1798. The general brought a group of artists and savants with his army, and before Admiral Nelson destroyed the French fleet in Aboukir Bay, these scholars made detailed studies of numerous temples and tombs. The interest generated by the impressive *Description de l'Egypte* (1809) and by the translation of the Rosetta Stone in 1821 spurred further expeditions and anthropological studies. This lure of things Egyptian also encouraged outright looting, as European treasure hunters amassed collections for private buyers and museums in London, Paris, New York, and Berlin. Nightingale refers to the availability of antiquities when she apologizes to her family for a lack of presents: "I thought in England one had nothing to do but walk into the tombs and dig out *the newest jewellery!*" (*Egypt*, 152).

When Nightingale arrived in Alexandria on 19 November 1849, a voyage on the Nile was not without its dangers. She saw several boats and their passengers lost in storms and hazardous passages through the cataracts. The government of Viceroy Abbas was showing signs of strain—

Abbas's own slaves revolted against his abuses and murdered him in 1854. All men were subject to conscription in the army, and Nightingale reported that mothers regularly lamed and blinded their male children in hopes of saving them from the draft. Yet visitors were assured that the viceroy used his brutal tactics to protect foreign visitors and their property from harm, and tourist trade was brisk; the period between 1830 and 1860 was "probably the high point of admiration in Europe and the United States of the culture of the Ancient Egyptians."[10] Nightingale complained that the "ruck" of English boats gathered below the cataract at Aswan had left "nothing to eat, for they had devoured everything like locusts" (*Egypt,* 120). These European travelers were enjoying the mild African winter while avoiding the unrest on the continent. Indeed, *Punch* noted in 1848 that "unless peace comes to the Continent soon . . . the Pyramids will be the only perfect substitute for Baden-Baden. . . . As peace and quiet are indispensable to the full enjoyment of a holiday, nothing nearer than the Pyramids can be thought of, at present, by travellers for pleasure."[11] Tourists were aided by the Peninsular and Oriental Steam Navigation Company, which had opened an overland rail route from the Suez to Cairo in 1842. After reaching the river, Nile excursions were offered on steamships, as well as the wind- and oar-powered *dahabiehs* used by the Bracebridge party. The state of mid-Victorian travel in Egypt can be judged by John Murray's guidebook, *A Handbook for Travellers,* which carefully notes "Things that should be Bought in England for the Nile Journey." The comprehensive list includes an umbrella, a sidesaddle, and a 27-volume library. The guide notes items that can be purchased more cheaply in England, but by 1858 Egyptian vendors were increasingly able to supply provisions for tourists: the book observes that "a man *may* take nothing more with him than he does in travelling on the Continent."[12] Nightingale and the Bracebridges arrived in Egypt with the requisite equipment, which included innumerable books on Egyptology and an ingenious mosquito-net sleeping arrangement called the "Levinge." Nightingale appreciated the comfort provided by her Levinge and described herself craftily distracting marauding insects before dashing to safety under the protective muslin.

The levity of Nightingale's letters was for the benefit of her family, but it belied her true condition. This vacation was not the life-affirming frolic in Rome, the city where she felt a little closer to heaven: Instead, it was a dark night of the soul. The strain of battling her family, of being denied professional training, and of abandoning the prospect of marriage had taken their toll. Nightingale's agitation began to take the form of "dreaming": "She fell into trances in which hours were blotted out; she lost sense of time and place against her will. In daily life she moved like an automaton, could not remember what had been said or even where she had been" (*Florence*, 51). She feared for her sanity. In this distraught state, Nightingale toured a country that she described as "a land of graves—amidst death and a world of spirits," an experience that suffered in comparison to her joyful Roman memories (*Egypt*, 168). As if to show that she was following instructions, Nightingale dutifully reported expeditions to her family, relating amusing anecdotes about donkey rides and her tour of the pyramids. Yet the stark beauty of Egypt was, to her, both solemn and forbidding, and the seeming normalcy of her letters is undercut by her anguished diary.[13] The detail in Nightingale's letters from Egypt allows them to be read as informative travelogues, but on another level, the private text records her despair down the length of the Nile. Her diary reveals a solitary battle against "self-will" and personal pride that must be fought before she can pursue her spiritual vocation.

Nightingale's first letter from Alexandria is reminiscent of her arrival at Rome, where she rushed to St. Peter's and imagined herself in the presence of God. In Egypt, it is the sunlight, "transparent and pure," that reminds her of heaven (*Egypt*, 21). The English sun is a mere lamp compared to the "living" light of Egypt: "[I]t is as if each ray was a messenger, alive" (22). Like St. Peter's, which welcomed her to Rome and seemed to bless her visit, the Egyptian "living" light seemed a benison to Nightingale.

In contrast to her Roman blessing, Nightingale's introduction to the East quickly became unsettling. At her request, the Egyptian consul arranged an "unprecedented" tour of a mosque. After donning the appropriate costumes and being warned not to show their hands, the Bracebridge party entered an Islamic house of worship. The Christian infidels were quickly spotted: "[T]he people crowded round us, laughing and pointing. I felt so degraded, knowing what they took us for, what they felt towards us. I felt like the hypocrite in Dante's hell with the leaden cap on—it was a hell to me. I began to be uncertain whether I *was* a Christian woman, and have never been so thankful for being so since that moment. That quarter of an hour seemed to reveal to one what it is to be a woman in these countries, where Christ has not been to raise us. . . . I was so glad when it was over. Still the mosque struck me with a pleasant feeling" (*Egypt*, 26). Nightingale recovered the composure of Western superiority, pitying the status of women confined to Eastern harems; her letter continues by detailing the mosque's activities with a tourist's eye, noting the basket makers and storytellers in the temple. But for a moment, the experience was disorienting. Her costume and attempts to hide her identity failed; by her intrusion into the mosque, Arabs assumed she was an unchaste woman and met her with derision. In this specifically non-Christian site, Nightingale was powerless to stop her audience's laughter, and she began to doubt herself. If a *Christian* woman would not be subject to such treatment, then who was she? The answer seemed to be that she was a Christian woman in hell.

Nightingale's first visit to a mosque, detailed in her first letter from Egypt, showed the conflict between East and West that proved profoundly disturbing to her. In other descriptions, she recorded a greater appreciation of the Eastern perspective. When she returned to a mosque at the end of her visit, the worshipers' reaction was similarly indignant. Again, she resisted being classified as a "Christian female dog," but her response at journey's end was more thoughtful: "It is exactly as if a dancer were to come, in her disgraceful dress, into Salisbury Cathedral, during the time of service" (*Egypt,* 197). Nightingale greatly admired Muslim charity, which required believers to give freely to any who asked, and she described the "very pretty" custom of honoring the dead by providing water to travelers (199). The architecture of Cairo, "the rose of cities," charmed her, and she found Arab inheritance laws much fairer to women than English ones (32). Yet for Nightingale, modern Egypt was at best a distraction from the land of the pharaohs: "Without the past, I conceive Egypt to be utterly uninhabitable" (139).

Through the intensity of Nightingale's rejection of Islamic Egypt, we can read the subtext of her holiday letters. During the course of her trip down the Nile, Nightingale fought off despair as her nursing vocation threatened to be postponed indefinitely. Egypt becomes increasingly evil as she ponders the seemingly insurmountable conflicts that prevent her from taking up her nursing project. Some of her strongest language, though, is evoked by the spectacle of suffering and powerlessness. As she describes a child being beaten by a police officer, she offers an almost tender description of the boy's white turban, which "came undone, and streamed upon the wind." Juxtaposed against the floating cloth, "the bastinado stick appeared: the Secretary (our friend) tried to interfere, but could do nothing. It made one quite sick, as all the details of government do in this horrid country" (*Egypt,* 36). The battered boy is unable to defend himself from the source of his misery. His vulnerability is obscene and must be condemned in the strongest terms. In "this hor-rid country" Nightingale witnessed meaningless pain, casually inflicted: she must have found painful parallels with her inability to command the events of her own life.

Nightingale's inner conflicts inform much of her horror at "uninhab-itable" Muslim Egypt, yet her descriptions of the East are typical of travel literature of the time. Western tourists, in their zeal to separate themselves from Eastern peoples, could even deny "that the Muslim inhabitants of modern Egypt, whether Arabian, Nubian, Turkish or Albanian, are human at all" ("Death," 98). Nightingale's letters show a clear bifurcation of Christian and infidel, living and dead, human and nonhuman. Looking at the Alexandrians' tiny huts, Nightingale can "hardly believe they are human dwellings" (Egypt, 25). As her trip pro-gressed and she viewed modern Egypt from Alexandria to Nubia, she was horrified by the contrast of ancient, ruined splendor and the "moral degradation" of modern Egyptians (81). She was particularly appalled by the Arab custom of building dwellings and villages within ancient tombs. Her European sensibility could not account for the ways in which Egyptian housing shaped itself to a harsh environment and adopted available materials. Off Hermonthis, downriver of Thebes, she described the contrast of "those columns lifting heads to the sky even now, when half buried, and carrying one's eyes naturally on high, and to see human beings choosing darkness rather than light, building their doorways four feet high or less, choosing to crawl upon the ground like reptiles, to live in a place where they could not stand upright, when the temple roof above their heads was all they needed!" (81).

Nightingale was drawn to the mysteries of the ancient pharaohs' religion, but modern Egyptians were to her inexplicably savage. She described the Ottoman Turks' government of Egypt as a system in which "little Beys [governors] have great Beys upon their backs to beat them, and great Beys have greater Beys, and so ad infinitum" (Egypt, 124). She observed repeatedly that order was maintained through the corporal punishment of the "bastinado," or cudgel. In Italy, she had fol-lowed every facet of papal reform; in Egypt, she claimed that politics were irrelevant "when it seems to matter so little. . . . In Italy one felt they were children, and their dawn was coming; here one feels as if they were demons; and their sun was set" (39). Nightingale had seen the poverty of Roman hospitals, which were often filthy and seemingly inhuman institutions. Yet in the East, she was repulsed by the "degrada-tion" of well-fed children; indeed, she noted that their British counterparts could not afford Egyptian diets that often included butter, chicken, and turkey. Two important differences separated the beggars of Rome and London from the villagers Nightingale saw along the Nile: their religion and their color.

In Rome, Nightingale looked beyond Catholic and Protestant distinctions to appreciate different varieties of devotion. She shows significantly less appreciation, though, for the unchristian. Christian beggars are poor but human; Islamic urchins are demonic. Her description of Ethiopian slaves on the Upper Nile portrays a group of young girls as ghoulish: "[T]hey came to beg of us, and, in the dusk, looked like skulls, with their white teeth; they set up a horrid laugh when we gave them nothing; our guide poked one with his stick, when *it* was sitting down, as if *it* were a frog" (*Egypt*, 88, emphasis mine). The *it*, a slave prodded with a stick, has ceased to be human. Her description of slaves on the Nile is markedly different from that of European "galley slaves" she saw in Rome. There, "slaves" were most likely convict laborers, but Nightingale found the sight of them working in chains to be "painfully disagreeable" (*Nightingale in Rome,* 56).

Nightingale's image of the East is no more or less racist than that of other tourists of her age. When confronted with the frightening differences of an African (non-European), Muslim (non-Christian), Arab (non-Caucasian) culture, many travelers developed a "genocidal fantasy": Europeans avoided the discomfort of negotiating cultural difference by simply wishing away Egyptians themselves ("Death," 119). When Nightingale despaired of the Egyptians enacting change through politics, she observed that "the sooner people are put out of their pain the better" (*Egypt,* 39). Off the island of Elephantine, she described a group of Nubian children who shyly watched the landing party. Nightingale observed that the dark-skinned children were not suffering; they "were not thin or starved." The difficulty was that they were the wrong color of black: running and stirring up dust, they were "not shiny as savages *ought* to be, but their black skins are dim and grimed with sand." Nightingale's charity could not encompass this heathen, brownish-black "troop of jackals": "I heard some stones fall into the river, and hoped it was they, and that that debased life had finished. . . . I gave them all the pins I had; it was all one could do for them" (86–87). For Nightingale, the children's accidental death would have been their kindest fate. Her European standards for charity are revealed in a discussion of a child at the island of Bidji. Nightingale is appalled by the custom of betrothing children, by the child's nakedness, and by the island women's general lack of religion. After a single encounter with the child, she suggested a plan to "take her and educate her, and send her back to educate the island" (117).

Just as Nightingale saw Egyptian natives through Western eyes, she compared Egyptian religion to the Roman Catholic models she had so recently witnessed. For Nightingale, the tombs of Beni Hassan, which were covered with depictions of the wealthy men buried there and scenes from their daily lives, represented a striking contrast to the Sistine Chapel: "[T]he one all ideal and aspiration, disdaining art and earth . . . the other, adhering with the most scrupulous fidelity to truth and exactness in real life—so that, at a distance of 4000 years, it is of infinitely more value to us than if it had been less literal" (*Egypt,* 55). Her analysis of prosaic Egyptian art was charmingly homey: "I think the Egyptian must have been very much like some of the English clergy wives of the present day, who preach out of the Old Testament and make muslin curtains." She found the "thoughtful metaphysical" Egyptian religion generally more philosophical than the "fervent" Catholic faith. According to Nightingale, within the intricate maze of columns of the Karnak temple at Thebes, "you think." In the open spaces of St. Peter's, by contrast, "you feel" (145).

Ipsambul, now known as Abu Simbel, appears to have been a literal and metaphoric turning point for Nightingale, as she realized that she was now going home. After the dangerous and "delightful" ascent of the cataracts (*Egypt,* 91), the party reached its southernmost point at the impressive Nubian temple of Ramses II. Here, they toured both the temple of the goddess Hathor and the Great Temple, with its four massive colossi, 66 feet high, hewn out of a cliff. Nightingale was moved by the carving over the temple entrance, in which Ramses offers the sun god not sacrifices but the figure of justice. Although she had been suitably impressed by the palaces at Thebes, Nightingale "can fancy nothing greater" than the temples of Ipsambul.

At her journey's apogee, just before the group began its return to Cairo, Nightingale found that "Egypt is beginning to speak a language to me even in the ugliest symbols of her gods, and I find there such pleasant talk—philosophy for the curious, comfort for the weary, amusement for the innocent" (*Egypt,* 104). She had found little common ground with the religion of Islam, but Ramses' tomb, where the great king is crowned by both good and evil, may have clarified for Nightingale why she had experienced delays and opposition in pursuing her vocation. Her diary declares that God delayed her trip to Kaiserswerth in order to teach her patience: "God told me what a privilege he had reserved for me, what a preparation for Kaiserswerth in choosing me to be with Mr. B[racebridge] during his time of ill health. . . . If I were never thinking of the reputation, how I sh'd be better able to see what God intends for me" (*Ever Yours*, 42). At Ipsambul, the message of accepting both good and evil was written large on the pharaoh's tomb, moving Nightingale to write, "What a deep philosophy! . . . The evil is not the opposer of the good, but its *collaborateur*—the left hand of God, as the good is His right" (*Egypt*, 96).

The "absolute solitude" of Ipsambul intensified its effect; throughout the trip, Nightingale described incidents in which villagers turned out to follow the tourists, "the whole population being there to hoot at you" (*Egypt*, 106). The grandeur and seclusion of Ipsambul earned Nightingale's highest praise. She found that "the temple of Ipsambul is the only thing which has ever made an impression upon me like that of St. Peter's," and in a letter dated 17 January 1850, she stated that "I never thought I should have made a friend and a home for life of an Egyptian temple, nor been so sorry to look for the last time on that holiest place" (105).

The praise of Ramses' tomb found in Nightingale's correspondence carefully concealed the private, personal struggle that her diary recorded. On 16 January, she "made a vow in the sacred place" of Ipsambul (*Study*, 156). Presumably this vow, like the vows she made in Rome, renewed her commitment to her nursing vocation. On 21 January, Nightingale sent her parents more travel details and a clever account of her pets, three "quarrelsome" chameleons. The next day, her diary recorded that "sitting on Philae by the temple of Isis, with the roar of the cataract, I thought I should see *Him. His* shadow in the moonlight in the Propylaeum." Unlike the image of Christ she saw before entering Rome, this holy vision did not seem to have provided comfort and assurance. On 26 January, her diary reported that she had "spoilt" the previous day's sight-seeing "with dreaming." She tersely added, "Disappointed with myself and the effect of Egypt on me. Rome was better." The letters from Nightingale's return passage recorded the charms of the islands of Philae and her particular affection for the toppled statue of Ramses II. She states that "Memphis has wound itself round my heart—made itself a place in my imagination" because of its gracefully "sleeping" colossus and the area's place in biblical history (*Egypt*, 172). Yet her diary told another story. Her entries recorded an ongoing conversation with God about her postponed vocation, a conversation often relayed through the Madre Santa Columba, her Roman spiritual advisor. On 28

February, "God called me with my Madre's words." On 1 March, Nightingale noted the anniversary of her retreat at the convent "two years ago!"
and despaired at how little progress had been made since that time. Six
days later, "God called me in the morning and asked me would I do
good for Him alone without the reputation?" (*Study*, 156). Nightingale's
diary describes the recurrent theme of quelling personal pride, an inner
struggle on a solitary Egyptian battleground: "Stood at the door of the
boat looking out upon the stars and the tall mast in the still night
against the sky (we were at anchor—they were all asleep and I could not
go to bed) and tried to think only of God's will, and that everything is
desirable and undesirable only as He is in it or not in it—only as it
brings us nearer or farther from Him" (157).

The diary indicates that Nightingale reviewed the notes taken from
her Roman retreat and focused on the question the madre presented to
her there: "Can you give up the reputation of suffering much and saying
little?" (*Study*, 157). Her inner distress and "dreaming" seem to have
mounted, since in March she reports that "God has delivered me from
the great offence and the constant murderer of all my thoughts" (*Florence*, 53). Her letters home continued to tell amusing stories of English
society along the river and at Shepheard's Hotel. The turmoil of her
diary, though, illuminates the hostility of her advice when the party
returned to Cairo: "Let no one live in the East, who can find a corner in
the ugliest, coldest hole in Europe" (*Egypt*, 176). Her rejection of the
East, with its devilish children and wretched animal-like inhabitants, is
a further manifestation of her emotional misery.

One of the few experiences that seemed to lift Nightingale's spirits
was her acquaintance with the Sisters of St. Vincent de Paul, who operated a school and hospital in Alexandria. Her visits with the sisters were
so frequent that "I was like a tame cat there, I went in without ringing,
and straight to the dispensary" (*Egypt*, 205). The comfort of the Catholic
convent was utterly consistent with Nightingale's spiritual aspirations.
Working with holy women who had already pledged themselves to God
must have made her own great work seem closer at hand. Whereas
Nightingale's descriptions of the Nile could be dismal, at the convent,
she said, "we were all very merry together." Not surprisingly, her diary
briefly loses its tortured tone. On April 1, she reported, "Not able to go
out but wished God to have it all His own way. I like Him to do exactly
as He likes without even telling me the reason" (*Florence*, 53). In the
comforting, familiar environment of the convent, she could more easily
endure the uncertainty of her mission.

The Bracebridges returned to England through Athens, and Nightingale's correspondence from that time described the Greek rebellion against the Turks. While her letters home engaged in political issues, Nightingale also sought out charitable workers to learn about their establishments. In Athens, she visited the orphanage and school of American missionaries John and Frances Hill, giving detailed accounts of the Greek refugee children she encountered there.[14] Her letters did not report, though, that she had begun to experience visions. At the Pass of Thermopylae, the site of the ancient Spartans' heroic loss to the Persians, rainbowlike "spirits" addressed the doubts that had haunted her throughout her journey. The voices told her that "life is a battle—a struggle against the principle of evil both in thine own soul and in the world—Christ is [the Spartan leader] Leonidas, this world is our Thermopylae" (*Study*, 163). In June, her diary records visiting the cave of the Eumenides to ask God the reason for her torment. She wrote, "Oh what is crucifixion—would I not joyfully submit to crucifixion, Father, to be rid of this. But this long moral death, this failure of all attempts to cure" (*Florence*, 54). Unable to act on her religious convictions or to begin the work she envisioned, Nightingale saw her condition as hopeless. The diversion of travel had been an utter failure, since "it little matters where I go—sold as I am to the enemy—whether in Athens or in London, it is all one to me" (*Egypt*, 54).

Nightingale's diary records a depression so serious that it threatened her health, and her condition only worsened as the travelers drew closer to home. In mid-June she recorded that "after a sleepless night physically and morally ill and broken down, a slave—glad to leave Athens. I had no wish on earth but to sleep." By the end of the month she was spending much of her time in bed, and her faint, shaky handwriting declares, "I cannot write a letter, can do nothing." The next day, she bleakly uttered, "I lay in bed and called on God to save me" (*Florence*, 54). At some point in their journey, the sympathetic Bracebridges made a critical decision to ease their charge's misery. The party would return to England through Germany so Nightingale could finally attend the Kaiserswerth Institution. This simple logistical change would allow Nightingale to gain the training she had sought since 1845, when her family scuttled her plans to visit Salisbury Infirmary. Yet her hopes had been raised so often that Nightingale refused to find comfort in this new prospect. In Dresden on 7 July, she feared that she would succumb entirely to "dreaming," writing that "it is rapidly approaching the state of madness when dreams become realities" (*Life*, 1:92). Two days later, she reviewed her life with resignation, reminding herself of the choices that had been available to her: those of wife, author, or "Hospital Sister." In a voice of surrender, she humbly claimed that "now it seemed to me, as if quiet, with somebody to look for my coming back, was all I wanted" (*Florence*, 55).

Until she actually saw Kaiserswerth, she would not believe that her much anticipated visit would transpire. But her spirits and her health improved dramatically when she reached the deaconess institution on 31 July. On reaching the Rhine, she felt herself to be a pilgrim, and she claimed the German river was "dearer to me than the Nile" (*Life,* 1:92). The Bracebridges arranged their travel to allow Nightingale a two-week introduction to the training facility; they stayed another fortnight to allow her to write "The Institution of Kaiserswerth on the Rhine," a pamphlet she later published anonymously that endorsed the organization. The woman who had seen visions, heard voices, and feared for her sanity recovered entirely as she worked among the nurses at Kaiserswerth. On 13 August, her diary stated she "left Kaiserswerth feeling so brave as if nothing could ever vex me again." Nightingale's bravery was short-lived; the vexations she fled would return when she rejoined her family. The Nightingales had hoped their daughter's travels abroad would provide an alternative to her persistent interest in nursing, a persistence that was making their lives together increasingly difficult. Instead, her trips only confirmed her interests and her need for meaningful work. Trips to Rome and Egypt had distanced her from family tensions, but a full-blown family crisis could not be diverted—only postponed.

Chapter Three
Reflections from the Daughter at Home: "Cassandra" and *Suggestions for Thought*

On her return from Egypt in 1850, Nightingale spent two weeks at the Kaiserswerth Institution in Germany. Her trip allowed her to inspect the nursing institution, but the visit was too brief to provide extensive training. During the short stay, Nightingale was greatly moved by the useful work and fellowship she found at this deaconess training house. Her inscription in the album of the director's daughter shows her gratitude: "Fl. N., die mit überfliezendem Herzen sich immer der Güte all ihrer Freunde in lieben Kaiserswerth irinnern wird. Ich bin ein Gast gewesen, und ihr habt mir beherbergt. [Florence Nightingale, who always will remember with an overflowing heart the good of all her friends at dear Kaiserswerth. I was a guest and you gave me shelter.]" (*Life,* 1:92).

The short tour of Kaiserswerth relieved the suffering she had endured in Egypt and renewed her faith in her nursing vocation. She still lacked her family's approval, though, and she returned home to find Fanny and Parthe as opposed to her nursing plans as they had been when she left. In addition, they were so scandalized by her hospital visit that they apparently invented a more respectable tale for family and friends. A thinly veiled autobiographical account later describes a woman "returning from the East, [who] had remained some weeks in a foreign institution for training deaconesses." An embarrassed relative prepared a cover story, explaining that "[i]t is rumoured in London that Miss —— remained on the Continent for the purpose of recovering her complexion before her return to England."[1] Her family's impassioned objections to the Kaiserswerth visit quickly reversed its positive effects on Nightingale's mental and physical health.

Parthenope was outraged at her sister's interest in nursing, afraid that her sister would abandon her for the sake of an unfashionable charity. As Florence showed increasing dissatisfaction with the restrictions of family life, Parthe clung ever tighter to her "with jealousy disguised as passionate devotion."[2] To compensate for her long absence during the Egyptian trip, the family determined that Florence would spend six months at home with Parthe. "To this I acceded," Nightingale later wrote. "And when I committed this act of insanity had there been any sane person in the house he should have sent for Connolly [a brain disease specialist] to me" (*Florence,* 57). Until April 1851, Florence would be her sister's companion, participating in the social and domestic activities that had always driven her to despair. The result was disastrous. The habitual "dreaming" that Nightingale had struggled with in Egypt returned; she compared it to "gin drinking" and claimed it was "eating out my vital strength" (58). With more than three months remaining in her family contract, Nightingale was suicidal. "I have no desire now but to die," a private note recorded on 30 December 1850. "There is not a night that I do not lie down in my bed, wishing that I may leave it no more." Her journals record the tedium of the family circle, describing "evenings that seem never to end—for how many long years I have watched that drawing room clock & thought it never would reach the ten & for 20 or so more years to do this" (*Ever Yours,* 44).

During this period, Nightingale declared, "My life is more suffering than almost any other kind, is it not, God?" (*Ever Yours,* 48). To cope with this misery, she started a spiritual autobiography that addressed issues of theology, sociology, and economics. Critics generally agree that plans for a three-volume project were made during 1851 and 1852. The idea for the project's first volume grew from Nightingale's experience, in the late 1840s, of nursing patients from the Derbyshire working class. This volume, dedicated to England's "artizans" proposed to discuss a new religious philosophy aimed at battling their atheism, a concern based in part on an 1851 census that revealed less than 25 percent of the population in large manufacturing districts attended church. A second volume that Nightingale originally titled "A Short Account of God's Dealings with the Author" would research religious psychology. The final volume would explore morality and God's law. By the end of 1852, she completed a 65-page proof, which she had privately printed.

After this beginning, Nightingale put the work aside and did not take it up again until after her return from the Crimea. In this revision, she expanded her 65 pages into a rambling 829-page social and theological critique. The text is loosely organized and repetitive; perhaps in an attempt to reach an "artizan" audience, she frequently restates her arguments, and the third volume is almost entirely a summary of the previous text. An introductory note to the second volume says that "the same subjects have been differently (and not always consecutively) dealt with in several portions of this book. A feeling of their extreme importance has dictated . . . this course, which has rendered repetition, even to the frequent use of the same phraseology, unavoidable."[3] For Thomas Carlyle, the effect was merely confusing. When excerpts from *Suggestions* appeared in *Fraser's Magazine* in 1873, Carlyle compared them to "a lost lamb bleating in the mountain."[4]

During 1859 and 1860, Nightingale solicited the opinions of prominent thinkers and considered revising the manuscript for publication.[5] Benjamin Jowett, Regius Professor of Greek at Oxford, was impressed by the text's originality. He nevertheless advised against publishing it without improving its organization, softening its combative "antagonisms," and removing "irritation in the tone" of the text (*Florence,* 237). In contrast, John Stuart Mill was struck by the observations of such a privileged insider and called her account "a testimony that ought not to be lost."[6] He borrowed generously from Nightingale's personal experience as he wrote *The Subjection of Women* (1869), and she received anonymous credit when he noted that "a celebrated woman in a work which I hope will some day be published, remarks truly that everything a woman does is done at odd times."[7] Even Mill's encouragement, though, was not enough to move Nightingale to publication. By 1860 she was a Crimean veteran, a reform-minded heroine who was considerably removed from the miserable creature that had been her sister's compulsory companion. Although a few copies of *Suggestions* were privately printed and distributed, she never took time to revise the text according to Jowett's guidelines. Nightingale was no longer living in her parents' home, and she had moved beyond the emotional life documented in her text. She had poured her frustrations into *Suggestions*, and it had served its purpose.

Nightingale dedicated her examination of religion to England's "artizans," but her manuscript was directed toward England's daughters. As an unmarried daughter at home, Nightingale was keenly aware of her social and economic vulnerability, and she recognized the larger set of circumstances that had created her domestic imprisonment. A private note from this period entitled "Butchered to Make a Roman Holiday" puts her misery in its social context. It asserts that "[w]omen don't consider themselves as human beings at all. There is absolutely no God, no country, no duty to them at all, except family. . . . I know nothing like

the petty grinding tyranny of a good English family. And the only alle-
viation is that the tyrannized submits with a heart full of affection" (*Ever
Yours*, 54). *Suggestions for Thought* combats the "tyranny" of the family by
using logic and biblical authority. The ambitious, unfinished project
compiles evidence to justify Nightingale's dissatisfaction with domestic
life, to defend her decision to leave her family, and to propel her along
the path that would lead to Crimea.

The Unheeded Prophetess: The Essay "Cassandra"

Nightingale's best-known writing is "Cassandra," the short essay that
appears at the end of the second volume of *Suggestions*. Taking its name
from the Trojan prophetess who was destined to be disbelieved, "Cassandra" makes a powerful case for the liberation of Victorian daughters. It
argues that "passion, intellect, moral activity—these three have never
been satisfied in woman," and it depicts the frustration of women who
"play through life" because serious interests are not taken encouraged
(*Cassandra*, 208, 214). "Cassandra" effectively inverts the ideology of
conduct books, tracts Nightingale says women use "to persuade themselves that 'domestic life is their sphere' and to idealize the 'sacred
hearth' " (229). Nightingale's own experience of these texts included
reading aloud *Passages from the Life of a Daughter at Home* (1846) to her
father. She filled the margins with angry rebuttals to its assertions, such
as declaring, "Behold the handmaid of the Lord! *not* Behold the handmaid of correspondence, or of music, or of metaphysics!" (*Life*, 1:94).
Texts such as *A Daughter at Home* urge women "to take their personal
griefs to God and leave them there," a strategy, critic Janet Larson says,
"so patently a means of rendering them socially docile that references to
prayer in Victorian women's texts are often read as repressive."[8] Nightingale's revisionary text mocks the dynamic in which women could
complain only to God because men would be "irritated with women for
not being happy," affirming women's right to complain and enumerat-
ing the particular grievances imposed upon her by her family and class
(*Cassandra*, 205).

Nightingale's prophecy speaks to daughters of privilege, women she
depicts as prisoners of their family's elegant drawing rooms. In "Cassandra," daughters are slowly murdered by domestic boredom, and seemingly homey family encounters become depictions of torture. In a typical gathering, "[e]verybody reads aloud out of their own book or
newspaper—or, every five minutes, something is said. And what is it to

be 'read aloud to'? The most miserable exercise of the human intellect. Or rather, is it any exercise at all? It is like lying on one's back, with one's hands tied and having liquid poured down one's throat. Worse than that, because suffocation would immediately ensue and put a stop to this operation. But no suffocation would stop the other" (*Cassandra*, 213). In Nightingale's assessment, the most painful part of a daughter's existence is her inability to control her own time. She is at the mercy of her family's social calendar, and since women have "accustomed themselves to consider intellectual occupation as a merely selfish amusement," they consider it "their 'duty' to give up for every trifler more selfish than themselves" (211–12). Consequently, women's pursuits must only be conducted at "odd times." Daily interruptions are annoying under any circumstances, but they are maddening to a woman attempting to pursue a vocation. Nightingale argues that women can accomplish nothing of importance in the brief moments they can call their own: "How should we learn a language if we were to give to it an hour a week? A fortnight's steady application would make more way in it than a year of such patch-work. . . . If a man were to follow up his profession or occupation at odd times, how would he do it? Would he become skilful in that profession? It is acknowledged by women themselves that they are inferior in every occupation to men. Is it wonderful? *They* do *everything* at 'odd times' " (*Cassandra*, 218–19).

Unmarried daughters were at their mothers' beck and call, but married women's free time was even more scarce. Nightingale reports a married woman's wish that she "could break a limb that she might have a little time to herself" (*Cassandra*, 213). The essay's connection between poor health and extra time has special resonance for Nightingale, who experienced poor health in her adult life that assured her privacy would be respected. "Cassandra" observes that "[w]idowhood, ill-health, or want of bread, these three explanations or excuses are supposed to justify a woman in taking up an occupation" (212). Nightingale's analysis, combined with her convenient, inexplicable fevers and heart palpitations, suggests that she employed illness to wage her own war against "odd times."

For Nightingale, the sinister symbol of the drawing room represents the well-to-do society in which ornamental young women are on constant call, and she emphasizes daughters' disadvantages by comparing their leisure to their brothers'. "Cassandra" offers the example of a son whose mother requests him "to shine in some morning visit." The son interrupts his reading on this occasion but declares that "I came that you might not think me sulky, but I shall not come again." "For a young woman to send such a message to her mother and sisters," Nightingale exclaims, "how impertinent it would be!" (*Cassandra,* 212). Nightingale attempts to defamiliarize women's duties by depicting men performing these activities. The image of a room of men "reading little books" is ludicrous, she says, yet the same idleness appears normal for women: "If one calls upon a friend in London and sees her son in the drawing-room, it strikes one as odd to find a young man sitting idling in his mother's drawing-room in the morning. For men, who are seen much in those haunts, there is no end of the epithets we have; 'knights of the carpet,' 'drawing-room heroes,' 'ladies' men.' . . . Now, why is it more ridiculous for a man than for a woman to do worsted work and drive out every day in the carriage? Why should we laugh if we were to see a parcel of men sitting round a drawing-room table in the morning, and think it all right if they were women?" (211). To an observer, the women at these social gatherings might appear merely frivolous. Nightingale asserts, though, that these pleasant-looking women are often deeply dissatisfied by their lives of leisure. She compares their lack of meaningful work to mental starvation, exclaiming that "[t]o have no food for our heads, no food for our hearts, no food for our activity, is that nothing?" (220).

Nightingale's essay sounds a general clarion call to "Awake, ye women, all ye that sleep, awake! If the domestic life were so very good, would your young men wander away from it, your maidens think of something else?" (*Cassandra,* 229). The specifics of the text, though, give notice that it is the author herself who has awakened. Fanny and Parthe's charming soirees are visible behind Nightingale's assertion that "[t]he time is come when women must do something more than the 'domestic hearth,' which means nursing the infants, keeping a pretty house, having a good dinner and an entertaining party" (229). The text is true to its author's experience, too, in its depiction of the family's emotional dynamics. Readers acquainted with the Nightingales would instantly recognize their youngest daughter in her assertion that "[t]he family uses people, *not* for what they are, nor for what they are intended to be, but for what it wants them for—for its own uses. It thinks of them not as what God has made them, but as the something which *it* has arranged that they shall be. If it wants some one to sit in the drawing-room, *that* some one is to be supplied by the family, though that member may be destined for science, or for education, or for active superintendence by God, *i.e.*, by the gifts within" (216).

Nightingale's essay was so clearly autobiographical that Jowett suggested omitting some of its more telling details. "[I]f the reflections on the family took less the form of individual experience," he said, they would avoid "painful remarks" (*Jowett's Letters,* 4). In its earlier drafts, though, the complaints of "Cassandra" were even more immediate. The text begun in 1851 with that title was a novel in which a protagonist named Nofriani critiques women's position in society. In this early draft, the protagonist, who calls herself Cassandra, despairs of the "dreaming" that Nightingale, in her own experience, had compared to "gin drinking." Nofriani recalls that "[t]hus I lived for over seven years dreaming always, never accomplishing—too much ashamed of my dreams, which I thought were 'romantic,' to tell them where I knew that they would be laughed out, if not considered wrong. So I lived, till my heart was broken. I am now an old woman at thirty."[9] As Nightingale revised her text, she eliminated some autobiographical details such as the narrator's age, which was the same as her own. She also excised some of the text's more inflammatory passages. An early draft of "Cassandra" compared marriage to prostitution, asserting that "[t]he woman is often a prostitute as a wife. She prostitutes herself, if she has sold her person for an establishment, as much if she had sold it in the streets. She prostitutes herself, if, knowing so little of her husband as she does, she begin immediately, without further acquaintance, to allow him rights over her person. She prostitutes herself, later, if, against her own desire, she allows herself to be made the blind instrument of producing involuntary children" (*Novel,* 37). In its final draft, Nightingale's essay observes that a woman who marries for "an establishment" is in no way superior to "those we may not name." In place of the prostitution analogy, Nightingale substitutes satire. In a social marriage of convenience, she says, the couple are "no more man and wife for that than Louis XIV and the Infanta of Spain, married by proxy, were man and wife" (*Cassandra,* 226).

Nightingale's revision of "Cassandra" progressed through three stages, beginning as a novel with a female narrator, Nofriani. In an intermediate stage, "Cassandra" adopts the voice of the heroine's brother Fariseo, who reports of his sister's weary life, "she could do nothing . . . having ceased to live the intellectual life long before she was deserted by the physical life" (*Novel,* 30). In its final form as an essay, "Cassandra" shows gaps and sudden jerks that mark deletions and changes to this narrative. For example, the essay's closing section contains the deathbed speech of a "dying woman to her mourners"; in her final moments, a gifted young woman welcomes the "divine freedom" of her death (*Cassandra*, 232). Originally, this melodramatic speech was given by Nofriani. In the essay, though, the emotional declarations provide an inexplicably abrupt ending. The disjointed quality of "Cassandra" is not the only result of Nightingale's three-step revision of the work. Nightingale effectively translated her text from a "female" genre—the novel—to a form perceived as more "masculine" and authoritative—the essay.[10] The attempt, whether successful or not, indicates that she was utterly serious about delivering her message.

Suggestions for Thought: *Practical Deductions* for the Victorian Daughter

The interest of feminist critics has made the essay "Cassandra" the most accessible and widely discussed of Nightingale's writings, but its place within *Suggestions for Thought* is less well-known. "Cassandra" concluded the work's second volume, an examination of social issues that Nightingale had renamed *Practical Deductions*. Because of Nightingale's practice of restating her ideas throughout *Suggestions*, *Practical Deductions* raises many of the issues later discussed again in "Cassandra," particularly Nightingale's critique of the family. In *Practical Deductions*, the claustrophobic upper-class family is described almost as a women's penitentiary: it is "smallest of all possible spheres, which will exercise no single one of her faculties" (*Suggestions*, 108). The text bristles with images of incarceration. "The prison which is called a family, will its rules ever be relaxed, its doors ever be opened?" she asks (*Cassandra*, 119). Social gatherings are periods of isolated, "solitary confinement": "[T]o be alone is nothing, but to be without sympathy in a crowd, this is to be confined in solitude" (149).

The lack of "sympathy" is what makes the family unit so intolerable, and *Practical Deductions* observes how little families know about their own members. Without this understanding, blood ties are "the iron chain . . . fettering those together who are not joined to one another by any sympathy or common pursuit" (*Cassandra*, 121). Nightingale complains that in an unnatural grouping of individuals with few common interests, daughters who long for meaningful work are isolated by a lack of understanding and simultaneously encroached upon by parents' meddling. She contends that "[w]e see parents building up obstacles in the way of their children as zealously as if it were their sole vocation!" (136).

Nightingale appreciates the difficult position of mothers in this dynamic, a situation she claims "requires the impossible. Before she was a mother she had no means of learning how to fulfil its requirements, and, if there were means, to learn or to practice all would be impossible" (174). Upper-class women never receive the training and preparation that would help them as mothers; they demand their daughters' care and attention without observing their daughters' needs. As a result, parents' claims for their daughters' duty are suspect. Nightingale dismisses their demands for care as further attempts at control: "The whole thing is a falsity! They don't want you to stay to take care of them . . . but for your own sake, for fear the world should think evil of you. . . . That parents should fancy that they can be benefitted, or that anybody else can be, just by the cramping of the daughters!" (145).

Observing the "cramped" position of daughters led Nightingale to draw fundamental conclusions about women's lack of autonomy. Parents' power is economic and legal power, and an unmarried daughter's only chance at independence is to outlive them; drawing on her own family's history of longevity, Nightingale grimly noted that daughters could be 60 years old before they came into an income. Her characteristic attention to specifics offers a detailed account of Victorian daughters' enforced penury. In well-to-do households, Nightingale complains, money is never forthcoming to endow unmarried daughters: "[P]arents live in such a way that they *must* say, 'We can spend 300*l* [£] a-year on a house in town, but we can't give anything like that to our daughters; it would be very inconvenient' " (*Cassandra*, 181–82). With relentless logic, Nightingale argues that parents should give daughters the income from their inheritance when they come of age, deducting household expenses if daughters continue to live at home. The cost to parents would be no more than a dowry, she claims, and she offers her figures for inspection:

> The Duke of ——— gave his daughters 10,000*l* when they married, that is 300*l*. a-year; they probably each cost him nearly that at home. Deducting their dress and maintenance, what would they have had left, even if he had given his single daughters the same as his married ones? Another rich man gave his daughter 5,000*l* when she married, that is 150*l* a year. If he had given her this when she came of age there would have been *nothing left, after deducting 100l* a year which he did give her for her dress, and what she cost at home. Most girls actually cost their parents as much at home as they do when they marry. (183)

Wealthy families control their daughters by effectively distancing them from ready cash, and at age 30, Nightingale balks at such infantilizing. *Suggestions* notes that parents fund only the projects that they approve, and it indicates that Parthe's requests for expenditures met with considerably more success than Nightingale's own: "[O]ne daughter, who chances to have the same tastes as her mother, may spend anything, because it falls in with the spirit of the family; and another, who has a somewhat differing turn of mind, nothing" (182). Nightingale observes that the law removes young men from such overprotective control by clearly stating that men will receive their property at age 21. The law intervenes in women's lives, Nightingale says, only to assure that their dowries are transferred safely from fathers to husbands.

Husbands offer young women their only hope of liberation, yet Nightingale's description of marriage is far from sanguine. "Cassandra" observes that courting is conducted in a drawing room where young people meet only *"to be idle"* (*Cassandra,* 224). Nightingale argues that the limitations of courtship ensure that women know dangerously little about the men they marry: "Unless a woman has lost all pride, how is it possible for her, under the eyes of her family, to indulge in long exclusive conversations with a man? 'Such a thing' must not take place till after her 'engagement.' And how is she to make an engagement, if 'such a thing' has not taken place" (224). In *Practical Deductions,* Nightingale observes that in a marriage market where a young woman is effectively "asking people to marry her all day long," successful marriages occur only by accident, and the union itself is trivialized (144). Marriages brokered in drawing rooms are, at best, only financial or social unions: "Mr and Mrs ——— unite together to keep up a political 'party,' and that is really more like love than most marriages, though it is only for party politics" (145). In "Cassandra," she observes that even this political marriage has more depth and meaning than the average match, and she paints a devastating portrait of superficial marriage that looks suspiciously like her own parents': "Husbands and wives never seem to have anything to say to one another. What do they talk about? Not about any great religious, social, political questions or feelings. They talk about who shall come to dinner, who is to live in this lodge and who in that, about the improvement of the place, or when they shall go to London. . . . But any real communion between husband and wife—any descending into the depths of their being . . . —do we ever dream of such a thing?" (222–24).

Nightingale consistently argues that women's happiness will arise from meaningful work, and she offers the same solution in her analysis of marriage. Individuals' interest in work would reveal their characters to potential mates and provide them a subject of mutual interest; the result would be happier unions: "When two meet each other at work upon an object interesting to both,—should not this be their introduction to love?" (*Cassandra,* 188–89). Mere physical and emotional attractions create marriages that cannot fulfill God's purpose; work, she argues, is the only firm basis for developing an equitable, spiritually satisfying union: "[T]hough there were differences in character, [if] there was interest for the same work, and *that good* work, then would there be a real independence for these two" (189).

Nightingale's analysis echoes her earlier decision to refuse Richard Monckton Milnes, a man she said could satisfy her intellect and passion but who would require a social life she could not provide. In a private note of 1849, she analyzes her refusal and determines that "I have a moral, an active, nature which requires satisfaction and that would not find it in his life. . . . I could be satisfied to spend a life with him in combining our different powers in some great object. I could not satisfy this nature by spending a life with him in making society and arranging domestic things" (*Florence,* 51). Nightingale outlines a strategy for meaningful, spiritually satisfying marriages among the upper classes, unions that transcend mere society matches by stressing philanthropy, work, and a precarious kind of independence. In the union Nightingale describes, a woman would, by law, remain financially dependent upon her husband; however, a couple could, "at each particular present, be independent in having each other's sympathy,—trusting for every other" (*Cassandra,* 189). *Practical Deductions* advances ideas about how such marriages can be formed, but it offers no examples. In Nightingale's theology, as in her personal life, such unions remained hypothetical.

"The Empirical Must Lead the Way to the Certain": Religious Notes for "Fellow Searchers"

When Nightingale rethinks the status of unmarried women, she asserts that her claims and intentions are utterly reasonable. "Why should any one be shocked at this?" she says. "What we have said amounts only to this, that unmarried women should have every facility given them by parents to spend their time and faculties upon any exercise of their nature for which it has an attraction, which can be pursued in harmony with God, which can answer, in short, any good purpose" (*Cassandra*, 163 – 64). Nightingale's assertion, made in the first volume of *Suggestions for Thought*, claims religious authority for revising unmarried women's roles. Her emphasis on the connection between religious and social discourse was a common one for Victorian women, whose society expected from them a degree of piety. Claiming religious authority illustrated a woman's devotion, but it also made good rhetorical sense: "Presenting themselves as prophets armed with scriptural authority, women could presume to construct their audience as sinners and define sinfulness in feminist terms: as tyranny over wives and daughters."[11] Nightingale argues that family and spiritual issues are bound by questions of agency and authority, "so intimately connected," she says, "that to ask concerning the higher power or powers acknowledged in heaven and on earth is one" (*Cassandra*, 156). Before Nightingale positions herself as the prophetess "Cassandra," then, *Suggestions* establishes her religious authority.

Victorian sages such as Thomas Carlyle warned audiences that they risked human health and happiness by abandoning the ways of God. Nightingale's message adopts this male tradition, and "in one stroke makes the sage's aggressiveness no longer the sole property of men."[12] Nightingale implicitly compares her observations to those of biblical prophets, whose difficult, unpopular observations she said were compelled by "a most deep and ingrained sense, a continual gnawing feeling of the miseries and wrongs of the world." The difference between the prophecies of Christ and those of modern women, she claims, is that women fail to act on the injustices that they identify. "The great reformers of the world turn into the great misanthropists, if circumstances or organisation do not permit them to act. Christ, if He had been a woman, might have been nothing but a great complainer" (*Cassandra*, 230). In the voice of a sage, Nightingale argues that the Fifth Commandment to honor one's father and mother is unjust because parents do not always earn their children's respect. She comprehensively corrects the biblical charge that one should "honor your father and your mother, so that you may enjoy long life in the Land which the Lord your God is Giving you." Nightingale finds that "[f]irst, we *can* only honour that which is honourable; secondly, filial piety has nothing to do with living to old age; thirdly, the Lord did not give them that land (in the sense in which Moses said it)—they took it" (*Suggestions*, 14).

Piety was encouraged in Victorian women, but biblical analyses and calls for social revision were not. Nightingale appropriates this privilege by adding the "masculine" authority of reason to the authority of religious devotion. Like Mary Wollstonecraft's *A Vindication of the Rights of Woman* (1792), which specifically rejects emotional "feminine" appeals while embracing "masculine" logic, Nightingale's text seeks to make its arguments appear realistic and objective. Although "Cassandra" makes emotional arguments that could be construed as "feminine," Nightingale uses empirical analysis to claim the authority of "masculine" reason. She draws on her confidence in statistics and fact, and argues for a logical religious faith. As long as religion operates at the level of illogical superstition and unscientific belief, she contends, no real moral progress can be made, and she complains that "*a priori* reasoning upon 'facts' which are not facts, begging the question upon foregone conclusions, is all the art or method we know" ("Interrogation," 577).

Nightingale claims that God's will, which she often refers to as "the character of God," can be revealed by examining evidence in the natural world. "Evidence may be brought of a will for a long time past active, in which we trace *some* benevolence, wisdom, power. But we are seldom called upon to act and feel by that of which we have certainty; we often have to act empirically," she claims. Nightingale trusts only the extrapolations made from reliable observations, arguing that "[t]he empirical must lead the way to the certain" (*Cassandra,* 11). Nightingale maintains, one critic argues, that "there is a necessary connection between empirical fact and rational truth and that this connection originates and derives its universality from God, the 'Lawmaker' " (*Victorian Women,* 203). Nightingale wants not the mystery of miracles but the guidance that arises from order. Until humanity can explain what she calls "the character of God," religion can have no direction. Without this knowledge, she protests, "how do we know where we are going?" ("Interrogation," 571).

Nightingale's empirical approach did not adhere strictly to any recognized religious creed—neither Catholic, Anglican, nor Evangelical. Instead, it was most closely aligned with the group of intellectuals who comprised the Broad Church movement. The nineteenth-century Anglican Church struggled to defend its beliefs against challenges from Darwinian theory and the German theology that questioned biblical accuracy. In contrast, Broad Church thinkers such as F. D. Maurice and A. P. Stanley called for freedom of inquiry in religious affairs, arguing that church doctrine should be held to the same critical standards as other scholarly endeavors such as science and history. During her family crisis of 1852, Nightingale considered converting to Catholicism, and *Suggestions* illustrates her knowledge of Catholic tenets. She praises Catholicism for the work it provided to women through religious orders. Her letters to the recently converted Henry Manning indicate how compelling she found holy orders. "If you knew what a home the Catholic Church would be to me! All that I want I should find in her. All my difficulties would be removed," she wrote to the future cardinal. After reading her philosophical manuscript, however, Manning refused to accept her conversion (*Florence*, 64–65). He pointed out how widely her beliefs varied from Catholic thought, particularly her stance on humility and obedience: "To 'esteem every one superior to ourselves,' would, if pushed to its ultimate practical consequences, become folly and untruth," Nightingale declares. "Then would a Galileo be seen giving up his opinion to any ignoramus" (*Ever Yours*, 95).

Nightingale never accepted the Catholic idea of submission. By the time *Suggestions* was revised in 1860, she had little sympathy for what she perceived as Catholicism's authoritarian repression of its followers or its mystifying, illogical belief in miracles. With an air of flippant finality, she declares that "with the God who carries about houses in the night and opens and shuts a picture's eyes, we can have no sympathy" (*Cassandra*, 197). Nightingale dismisses what she sees as Catholic superstition, but the power of the Church's devotion remains compelling. "The Roman Catholic idea is not nearly so fine as God's thought," she says, "[b]ut it is the *next* fine idea to it. If God had not done what He has done, He would have done what the Roman Catholics say He has" (*Suggestions*, 15).

Nightingale respected holy orders and the power of devout belief, but she observed that religion was riven with contradictions. With a mixture of logic and angry indignation, *Suggestions* takes aim at nearly every established sect. She perceives that the same questions exist in all religions, since "[e]xcept in religious orders, the Roman Catholic, the Puseyite, the Evangelical, the Jew, in the higher and middle ranks of life, live much after the same fashion . . . [and] their habits do not differ materially or generally according to their religious views" (*Suggestions*, 140). She neatly summarizes her difficulties with Christianity's two major branches by comparing them to earthly mothers. Catholicism is "over busy," and its tyrannical domesticity reads like a portrait of Fanny Nightingale: "*She* [Catholicism] imprisoned us; she read our letters; she penetrated our thoughts; she regulated what we were to do every hour;

she asked us what we had been doing and thinking" (*Cassandra*, 84). In contrast, the Church of England is an absentee parent much like W. E. N., who habitually retired to the safety of the Athenaeum Club when his home became a battleground. The Anglican church is an "over-idle mother, who lets her children entirely alone." Sharper criticism of the Anglican Church characterizes it as sterile and bourgeois, a religion of "order, decency, respect. It is probably much better than none: but of how much more is not humanity capable!" (*Suggestions*, 50). Raised in the Church of England, Nightingale knew where to look for its contradictions, and she finds particular fault with its nationalism. She condemns the Church's belief that God " 'hath set apart' the English for Himself, and favoured them to the detriment of every other nation" (9). As her scorn increases, her protest escalates to ridicule. "Two hundred years hence what will be thought of us? that we ought to have been in a lunatic asylum; but people in lunatic asylums are more sensible. Is it as extraordinary that a man should think himself a teapot as that we should think God like this?"

Although Nightingale finds fault generally with hypocritical religious institutions, analysis of the notorious "Gorham case" illustrates her challenge to a more particular Church doctrine. In a widely publicized controversy that began in 1848, George Gorham was denied an appointment to an Exeter parish because he did not subscribe to the Anglican stance on infant baptism. The Anglican belief in sin and regeneration was not clarified, but many interpreted it to mean that infants who died before baptism could not be saved from eternal damnation. Tractarians were horrified, and many converted to Roman Catholicism over the affair. Nightingale finds the decision barbarous, calling the idea of infant damnation a "superstition about the nature of God unparalleled for its atrocity in any savage tribe" (*Suggestions*, 87). Equally appalling, she thinks, is the casual indifference of a church "which embraces nearly all the cultivated men in the kingdom" to such an important doctrinal issue. With withering sarcasm, she characterizes the Church's response to Gorham: "[I]t was an open question whether babes who died unbaptized were damned or not. . . . [I]t did not signify—it might be so—men might believe one or the other, as they chose." As she explores the logic behind the decision, Nightingale finds the church's real failure to be in its method. In particular, she cites its failure to analyze the laws of moral philosophy and the concept of "justice": "[P]eople have said that 'God is just,' and have credited Him with an injustice such as transcends all human injustice . . . e.g. that He condemns to 'everlasting fire' for not being baptised little babies who certainly could not get themselves baptised. . . . But would God be the more just, even though He does not damn the little babies, if He does not *save* them—if he has no scheme by which the little babies, who were never asked whether they would come into this world or not, are to be brought into perfect happiness?" ("Interrogation," 574).

In addressing the Gorham controversy, Nightingale observes the inconsistency of a "just" God who condemns unbaptized infants. In her larger theology treatise, she finds the irrational idea of forgiveness as barbaric as the cruelty of damnation. Unexamined forgiveness, Nightingale believes, is useless: "What takes place when we are forgiven? Is it a change in God or in man? What is it?" In typical irascible form, she concludes that "[w]e know no more than if you were speaking Chinese" (*Suggestions,* 55). Although she disagrees with Calvinist ideas of predestination, Nightingale argues that acts requiring forgiveness arise according to God's plan. If the world adheres to a larger order, then mistakes are made for a reason; like Meister Eckhart, Nightingale believes that evil was an integral part of the divine plan because it allows humanity to learn from its errors. Because she views human fallibility as a diagnostic tool, Nightingale argues that God's justice cannot encompass the concept of eternal damnation: "We find that *punishment*, if the word be used in the sense of suffering or privation consequent on sin or ignorance, does not exist in God's moral government, and we see it to be right, because its effect will be sooner or later to induce mankind to remedy the evils which incur it. But eternal punishment, or vicarious punishment would be the satisfaction only of revenge, not of justice" (74).

Nightingale's theology reflects her assurance in a benevolent God and the perfectibility of mankind. In approaching theology as an ordered science like geology or astronomy, she predicts a moral evolution that will develop as civilization acquires "a more comprehensive, more impressive belief, as moral philosophy becomes fathomed by the understanding and raises the feelings" (*Cassandra,* 13). Her empiricism draws on Auguste Comte's agnostic positivism, the theory that later helped establish the modern field of sociology. Comte identifies stages of human development and argues that behavior conforms to universal laws; Nightingale adds to his empirical analysis the fervor and discipline of medieval mystics. She later would prepare translations of medieval visionaries such as the Blessed Angela of Foligno and St. John of the Cross, mystics who attract her with their ability to abandon "all that mechanism & liv[e] for God alone" (*Suggestions,* xiii). The discipline that draws Nightingale is not the mystics' tradition of renunciation; indeed, she holds that "to 'renounce worldly enjoyment' implies a mistake. It should be our enjoyment to do the world's work" (*Victorian Women,* 229). Instead, the qualities she admires in mystics such as St. Theresa are much like the ones she praises in Roman Catholic holy orders—"their absolute linking of themselves in the idea of service."[13]

Nightingale defines mysticism as "not devotion, but work and suffering for the love of God" (*Life,* 2:233). Of all her theological speculations, it is perhaps her emphasis on work that offers the most insight into her spirituality and her application of it to secular pursuits. Work provided her life with a center and a purpose; without it, she was the miserable creature who had toured Egypt like an automaton. It is characteristic, then, that her theology does not emphasize doctrine or passive prayer. Indeed, she mocks her childhood experience of the Anglican Litany, a period in which her prayers "asked for what I really wished, and really wished for what I asked. . . . How ill-natured it is, if you believe in prayer, not to ask for everybody what they want. . . . [But] I could not pray for George IV. I thought the people very good who prayed for him, and wondered whether he could have been much worse if he had not been prayed for. William IV, I prayed for a little. But when Victoria came to the throne, I prayed for her in a rapture of feeling, and my thoughts never wandered" (*Cassandra,* 57–58). As a child, Nightingale had prayed and then "wait[ed] for the answer as if I had been a servant, which I truly believed myself, sent on a message" (58).

In contrast, the adult Nightingale describes an active spirituality that finds its confirmation in work. She asserts that "man must create mankind," meaning that humanity must improve its moral condition by discovering God's laws.[14] "Creating mankind" and raising humanity's moral state also meant improving the material conditions that led to human suffering. The Litany requests God's aid, protection, and mercy, but it provides no vehicle for humankind to initiate God's plan. Nightingale notes the contradiction of such invocations when she recalls, "It did strike me as odd, sometimes, that we should pray to be delivered 'from plague, pestilence, and famine,' when all the common sewers ran into the Thames, . . . and the districts which cholera would visit could be pointed out. I thought that cholera came that we might remove these causes, not pray that God would remove the cholera" (*Cassandra,* 59).

The tome begun during Nightingale's domestic servitude clearly anticipates the tireless work that will characterize her life after serving in the Crimea. *Suggestions* stresses humanity's need to improve itself by learning God's laws, but equally important is the grace that arises from the act of labor. Nightingale writes to Jowett in 1862 "that it is a religious act to clean out a gutter and to prevent cholera, and that it is not a religious act to pray (in the sense of asking)" (*Jowett's Letters*, 18). Nightingale's focus on work as salvation may have arisen from her feelings of embattlement during the years that her nursing plans were delayed. She had no illusions that salvation or spiritual evolution was easy; indeed, a letter written in 1846 describes the process as a bitter campaign. To her aunt Hannah Nicholson, Nightingale declares that "life is no holiday game, nor is it a clever book, nor is it a school of instruction nor a valley of tears—but it is a hard fight, a struggle, a wrestling with the Principle of evil, hand to hand, foot to foot—every inch of the way must be disputed" ("Spirituality," 51). During the long years she waited for her ideas about nursing to be accepted, Nightingale had seen little evidence of miracles, except those achieved by the exacting compilation of data and sheer persistence. *Suggestions* reflects that struggle, declaring that "God *gives* us nothing. We are to work out a happiness, like His, in ourselves, in accordance with His laws" (*Suggestions*, 76).

Adopting the sage's voice of biblical authority allows *Suggestions for Thought* to reject women's passive, silent suffering. Nightingale asserts that God uses pain to indicate the need for earthly change, and her misery is God's message: "When I feel low, and poor and miserable in a drawing-room life, where I can do nothing, is not that His word to me, saying 'Now you see that in this life human nature is not exercised to anything like the degree which it is capable of. You feel very uncomfortable, therefore, change it as soon as you can' . . . Can He speak plainer than He does?" (*Cassandra*, 81). For readers of *Suggestions*, though, the size and scope of Nightingale's prophecy remains a challenge. Despite attempts to clarify her ideas through restatement, the universal law that appeared so logical to her remains maddeningly elliptical to others. Jowett took the liberty of a close friend to complain in 1872 that "[d]uring the ten years & more that I have known you, you have repeated to me the expression 'character of God' about 1,000 times, but I cannot say that I have any clear [idea] of what you mean, if you mean anything more than divine perfection" (*Jowett's Letters*, 234). John Stuart Mill took issue with Nightingale's confidence in a benevolent God who guides mankind toward perfection. He observed that "[t]here are many signs in the structure of the universe of an intelligent power wishing well to men and other sentient creatures. I could, however, show, not so many perhaps, but quite as decided indications of an intelligent power or powers with the contrary propensity" (*Suggestions*, 16).

Part of Nightingale's rhetorical difficulty arises from the combative posture she must take simply to make her claims for religious authority and the reassessment of the position of Victorian women. Prophetic speech like Nightingale's often produces "extremist rhetoric [and] distorting absolutes" as it battles the language of the dominant culture ("Lady Wrestling," 62). Jowett acknowledged this combative posture when he observed that readers of *Suggestions* would call Nightingale "an infidel who has been a Papist" (*Life*, 1:487). Nightingale's contribution to theological debate challenged Victorian sensibilities, but through her reinterpretation of religious discourse she proclaimed women's right to textual authority, denying the "societal restrictions of female interpretation by making such interpretations in the first place" ("Sage," 41). *Suggestions for Thought* remains a disjointed combination of theology and feminism, but in its sometimes uneven prose, it reveals the difficulty of the task Nightingale set for herself and the power that religion offered to Victorian women.

Prophecies Fulfilled: An End to "Poor Cassandra"

In her own life, Nightingale was not fated to be "poor Cassandra." After all her suffering, Nightingale's fortunes improved, in part because her six months' service to Parthenope helped clarify the means toward her vocation. In June 1851, only two months after finishing her domestic tenure, her private notes record, "I must *take* some things, as few as I can to enable me to live. I must *take* them, as they will not be given me; take them in a true spirit of doing Thy will" (*Life*, 1:107). Either her strong will or her family's weariness won the day: by July 1851, she had begun the long-awaited training program at Kaiserswerth. Fanny could not have received well the letters reporting that her daughter rose at 5 A.M. and had meals of rye tea and broth. Neither could she have celebrated her daughter's report that "the operation to which Mrs. Bracebridge alludes was an amputation at which I was present. I find the deepest interest in everything here, and am so well in mind and body" (1:112). Years later, Nightingale played down the training she received during her three-month stay, observing that "the hospital was certainly the worst part of Kaiserswerth" (*Florence*, 61). Its worth to her was the confidence and peace of mind it inspired.

This new element of confidence is briefly revealed in *Suggestions*, where Nightingale observes that "it is almost invariable that, when one of a family is decidedly in advance of all the others, he or she is tyrannized over by the rest, and declared 'quite incapable of doing anything reasonable'" (*Suggestions,* 104-5). Clearly, Nightingale is the family member with the advanced skills, and she would wait no longer for her family's acceptance. In one last letter from Kaiserswerth, she asks her mother to "[g]ive me time, give me faith. Trust me, help me. I feel within me that I could gladden your loving hearts which now I wound" (*Life,* 1:114). Her letter was never answered, and Nightingale's new approach was summed up in a note that declared bluntly, "There are knots which are Gordian and can only be cut" (*Florence,* 60).

Nightingale cut the Gordian knot with Parthe's unwitting assistance. In 1852, while Nightingale visited hospitals in Dublin, Parthe experienced a complete mental breakdown. The attending physician, Sir James Clark, noted that her "degree of chronic delirium" and "extreme irritability" had been, "I venture to say, fostered by over-indulgence." He recommended that Parthe break her dependence on her sister, a prescription that Nightingale believed ignored the underlying causes of the illness. She later reported that a "successful physician once seriously told a sister who was being Devoured that she must leave home in order that the Devouree might recover health and balance which had been lost in the process of devouring" (*Florence,* 66). Nightingale resented the culpability implied in Clark's diagnosis, but his recommendation provided her with an ironclad rationalization for leaving her family. She presented the issue gravely to Henry Manning. "If my dear parents cannot think it right to make the changes he prescribes, I hope that they will not blame me for withdrawing from taking part in a way of life in which I must either yield to my sister to her destruction (Sir James Clark having expressly stated that the brain is actually in a state of disease & that yielding to her must increase this state of the brain) or by opposition to her wishes & ideas I must be perpetually increasing her nervous excitement & fostering the monomania about me" (*Ever Yours,* 60–61). Nightingale may have been the only member of the family to take the doctor seriously: at the time of her letter, she reported that her mother and sister were planning their schedule of fall parties. Nightingale assumes an air of secrecy and heroism as she claims that "[i]t is only known that my sister has bad health & what I can be doing away from home, 'nobody *can* understand.' " Misunderstood or not, she acted on the opportunity her sister's poor health presented.

Nightingale continued her training by visiting nursing facilities abroad. Through her widening circle of friends and professional acquaintances, knowledge of her interest in nursing grew. In 1853, her friend Elizabeth Herbert announced that the Institution for the Care of Sick Gentlewomen in Distressed Circumstances needed a superintendent. The charity hospital was perfectly proper, as Nightingale noted, with "no Surgeon Students or Improper Patients there at all" (*Florence,* 70). The women of Nightingale's family raised their familiar complaints, but W. E. N. could bear no more weeping and raging. While Florence negotiated her appointment, her father retreated to the Athenaeum Club and drafted a note to Parthe. "Having come to the resolution that it is entirely beyond your mental strength to give up interference in your sister's affairs and being equally sure that your health cannot stand the strain," he said, "we advise you to retire from London and take your books and country occupations till her proceedings are settled." W. E. N.'s resolve failed, and the letter was never sent. Upon reflection, he decided that instead of chastising his older daughter, he would liberate his younger one. Acting on just the plan that Nightingale would advocate in *Suggestions*, W. E. N. gave her financial independence—£500 per year, even more than the Duke of ————'s daughter.

In August 1853, Nightingale began her work at the gentlewoman's institution on Upper Harley Street, London. The professional advancement was limited, but the administrative experience was illuminating. She raised standards for general cleaning and housekeeping. She installed more efficient facilities, placing hot-water spigots on each floor. She drew up new contracts for medicine and groceries, much to the institution's financial benefit. She battled the hospital's committee until it agreed to take in women of all religions. In short, she professionalized a poorly administered charity run by well-meaning amateurs. Perhaps her most important lesson concerned the institution's politics. She wrote her father in December 1853 that "when I entered into service here, I determined that, happen what would, I *never* would intrigue among the Committee. Now I perceive that I do all my business by intrigue. I propose in private to A, B, or C the resolution I think A, B, or C most capable of carrying in committee, and then leave it to them, and I always win" (*Life,* 1:135).

In her professional and private life, Nightingale had learned expediency and pragmatism. With her family, that meant summoning the discipline to maintain her hard-won independence. Mary Clarke Mohl chided Nightingale for not living with her family while they were in

London for the social season, but Nightingale emphatically defended her need for distance: "I have not taken this step, Clarkey dear, without years of anxious consideration. . . . I mean the step of leaving them. I do not wish to talk about it—and this is the last time I shall ever do so. . . . I *have* talked matters over ("made a clean breast," as you express it) with Parthe, *not once but thousands of times.* Years and years have been spent in doing so. It has been, therefore, with the deepest consideration and with the fullest advice that I have taken the step of leaving home, and it is a *fait accompli*" (*Life,* 1:138–39). At age 33, Nightingale severed the domestic bonds that caused her to doubt her sanity. If the decision was painful, the result was utterly satisfying. Her life was her work, as she had long declared it should be. In a January 1854 letter to her Aunt Hannah that discusses the "consolations" and "disappointments" of her nursing vocation, Nightingale reflects, "I have never repented nor looked back, not for one moment. And I begin the New Year with more true feeling of a happy New Year than ever I had in my life" (*Ever Yours,* 76).

Nightingale declares to Mary Clarke Mohl that she does not wish to talk about her decision to leave her family. Yet the anger, guilt, and resolution of that decision are thoroughly illustrated in *Suggestions for Thought.* This contentious, repetitious, and decidedly nonlinear text reflects Nightingale's distress over compulsory domestic life that had reached a peak during her servitude to Parthe. By the end of her six months of domestic imprisonment, Nightingale's guilt at disrupting her family had evolved into anger at her own victimization. By June 1851, she asserted that "it is impossible for any situation to go on well where one is at the bottom who ought to be either independent or at the top. I am at the bottom & ought not to be there" (*Ever Yours,* 49). The revisions, reiterations, and intensity of *Suggestions* show that, even for a woman of Nightingale's character and strength, concluding that she "ought not to be" on the bottom was enormously difficult.

Chapter Four

Notes on Matters Affecting the Health, Efficiency, and Hospital Administration of the British Army: The Crimea and Hospital Reform

After years of preparation and struggle, Nightingale gained a small but significant prize in 1853: a supervisory position at the Institution for the Care of Sick Gentlewomen in Distressed Circumstances. The supervision of servants, tradespeople, and convalescent governesses was hardly challenging, but it allowed her to begin work in her chosen field and provided independence from her family's interference. Yet after restructuring the nursing facility's administration, Nightingale observed that the Harley Street home offered only limited nursing experience. Her quarterly reports are filled with descriptions of minor housekeeping irregularities and troublesome charity patients who by "curious pathological fact" always "take to their bed on the third day after their admission."[1] The report of 20 February 1854 notes that "[t]here is not a trick in the whole legerdemain of Hysteria which has not been played in this house" (*Harley Street*, 15). When she filed a report six months later, Nightingale prepared the home's governing committee for her departure, saying that she had "done the work *as far as it can be done*, —it is probable that I may retire, *if*, in pursuance of my design & the allegiance which I hold to it, I meet with a sphere which is more analogous to the formation of a Nursing School" (35–36). Such a sphere had already presented itself: Nightingale was being considered for the superintendent of nurses position at King's College Hospital in London, a job that promised to provide much more challenging duties than her work with distressed gentlewomen. If appointed, her plan was to develop a facility, modeled on the Kaiserswerth Institution, that would train farmers' daughters to be nurses. Nightingale might have indeed built a career supervising farmers' daughters had circumstances not brought her into the national spotlight.

In 1853 Russian troops moved into territories east of the Black Sea, Moldavia and Wallachia, ostensibly to protect the Orthodox Christians living in that part of the Ottoman Empire. This occupation was less an issue of religion than a display of military posturing: Russia continued to search for a warm-water port, and the decaying Ottoman Empire appeared increasingly vulnerable. Great Britain and France, alarmed at Russian advancement, allied themselves with Turkey. Diplomatic negotiations failed, and on 28 March 1854, England joined its allies in declaring war on Russia. The Queen's forces, though, were scarcely up to the task, having been at peace—and underfunded—since the end of the Napoleonic wars. In addition, the army was comprised of regimental units that functioned almost independently of one another. Because officers paid hefty prices for their commissions, they were inclined to think of regiments as personal fiefdoms. The regimental organization raised problems enough, but a Byzantine system of transport and supply had been designed to prevent fraud, and basic provisions were delayed by complicated rules for requisitions. For example, the form for ordering a greatcoat contained two schedules with 24 blanks, to be filled out in duplicate; in addition, regulations specified that soldiers could order new coats only once every three years.[2]

In the Crimea, this system created intolerable conditions by clinging to administrative guidelines while ignoring the obvious. For example, the army had determined that soldiers who arrived in army hospitals would furnish many of their own supplies—including clothing and eating utensils—from their own knapsacks. This order overlooked the fact that many soldiers had been ordered to abandon their knapsacks to speed up troop movement. As months dragged on, no other steps were taken to outfit army hospitals, and sick soldiers arrived lacking necessities such as hospital gowns, soap, towels, and spoons. The entire army suffered from the failure to develop an adequate system of roads. When cart tracks became muddy bogs in winter, soldiers were deprived of food, fuel, and medicine. As a result, men starved, froze, and died by the score from preventable camp diseases, including cholera. Of the 21,000 men who died in the Crimean conflict, 16,000 died of disease rather than combat wounds. Officers who complained about the hardships created by these conditions were often risking their military careers. In February 1855, at the height of a cholera epidemic, Nightingale despaired that "among all the men here, is there one really anxious for the good of the Hospitals, one who is not an insincere animal at the bottom, who is not thinking of going in with the winning side, which ever that is?" (*Duty*, 82).

Deaths from disease, malnutrition, or exposure were not new in the military, but the invention of the telegraph allowed the public to read contemporaneously, for the first time, how wars abroad were conducted. Newspaper coverage of the army was so extensive and detailed that a Russian general was said to have claimed that "[w]e have no need of spies, we have the [London] *Times*."[3] By 9 October 1854 the British public began receiving accounts of military hospitals in Scutari, Turkey, a city across the Bosphorus from Constantinople. The *Times* reported that pensioners hired to serve as an ambulance corps were utterly failing. Transport ships brought the sick and wounded across the Black Sea from the Crimea to Scutari, where orderlies then carried invalids up the steep, muddy road that led from the bay to one of the three Scutari hospitals: the huge Barrack Hospital and the smaller General and Kulali hospitals. Correspondent William Russell reported that "[w]hether it was a scheme for saving money by utilizing the poor old men or shortening the duration of their lives and pensions, it is difficult to say, but they [orderlies] have been found in practice rather to require nurses themselves than to be able to nurse others."[4] Three days later, the newspaper described wounded men from the battle of the river Alma, just north of Sebastapol in the Crimea, arriving at the Barrack Hospital. The correspondent found that the bungled reception of 4,000 men "certainly reflects great disgrace somewhere or other. [W]e are told of patients lying for hours, and even days, and making desperate attempts to catch the surgeon in his flying visits from ward to ward. This great deficiency, great as it is, can scarcely be called the greatest. *There are no nurses at Scutari;* at least none for the English, though the French are attended by some Sisters of Mercy from a neighbouring convent. . . . [T]here is not even linen and lint to bind wounds" (emphasis mine).

Readers were incensed by Russell's accounts, and the more news they heard, the worse the story became. During Parliament's debate in January 1855, M. P. Bernal Osborne declared that the government must "lay an unsparing hand on that building adjacent to these premises—you must see whether, in fact, you can find a modern Hercules to turn the Serpentine through the Horse Guards and all the ramifications of the War Office."[5] Osborne's allusion to the Aegean stables proved to be particularly apt, because inadequate treatment of sewage contributed to a cholera epidemic that decimated the troops during the winter of 1854

to 1855. J. A. Roebuck called for a parliamentary committee to investigate the condition of the army, saying the question was "a simple matter
of figures." On the floor of Parliament, he declared: "It appears, then
that 14,000 men remain out of the whole 54,000. I want to know, Sir,
what has become of the 40,000 troops who have disappeared from the
ranks of your army" (*Hansard's*, 981).

Roebuck's Sanitary Commission, a group of physicians and sanitary
engineers, was given its orders on 19 February 1855 and soon went
abroad to review army hospitals. They reported that at Scutari, sewage
pipes drained into the sea, with sewer openings above sea level. This
design allowed wind to blow through the pipes and force sewage gases
back into the hospital, where nurses noticed a higher percentage of
fatalities occurring in patients whose beds were near toilet facilities. The
candid report of 6 March 1855 explains that soldiers had broken off the
privy taps used by the Turkish soldiers who previously occupied the barracks. Water was subsequently shut off, and sewer pipes quickly clog-
ged. A commissioner states that

> the liquid fæces, the evacuations from those afflicted with diarrhoea,
> filled up the pipes, floated up over the floor, and came into the room in
> which the necessaries were, extended and flowed into the ante-room, and
> were more than an inch deep when I got there in the morning; men suf-
> fering from diarrhoea, who had no slippers at the time and no shoes on,
> as this flood of filth advanced, came less and less near to the necessary,
> and nearer and nearer to the door, till at last I found them within a yard
> of the ante-room performing the necessary functions of nature; and in
> consequence the smell from this place was such that I can use no epithet
> to describe its horror.[6]

This unflinching account of hospital sewage is quoted in Nightingale's own report on her Crimea experience, entitled *Notes on Matters
Affecting the Health, Efficiency, and Hospital Administration of the British
Army* (1858). The events that took Nightingale to the Crimea and ultimately led to her creation of this 800-page account were made possible
by her preparation and social connections. Her interests in nursing and
hospital administration were well known; by great good luck, though,
she had a close friend in a key cabinet office. Sidney Herbert, whom she
had met in Rome, was now secretary at war. The day after William Russell complained that "there are no nurses at Scutari," Nightingale and
Herbert privately worked out details of an unprecedented nursing expedition. Her sister, Parthenope, reports that the two negotiated with

heads of nursing sisterhoods, women who initially wished to accompany their charges to the Crimea. With further discussion, "all gave way & Florence is sole leader."[7] By 14 October the secretary's proposal that Nightingale head a nursing party was a formality. Herbert's letter shows how much Nightingale's nursing expedition owed to the negative newspaper accounts and the incensed public's call for action. The secretary was confident that even Nightingale's family would approve of the decision because "the work would be so national, and the request made to you proceeding from the government who represent the nation comes at such a moment, that I do not despair of their consent" (*Life*, 1:153–54). Even a young lady employed with such "national" work required a chaperon; therefore, the Bracebridges, her companions in Rome and Egypt, agreed to accompany her. On 21 October Florence Nightingale departed for the Crimea with a party of 38 nurses and soon became an international heroine.

Her 18 months in the Crimea won her lasting fame as "A Lady with a Lamp." She was recognized throughout the world for her care of the common soldier, the wretch that the Duke of Wellington had condemned as "the scum of the earth enlisted for drink." Her respect for soldiers' dignity changed the popular conception of the Queen's army, and the troops adored her. A popular song of the period illustrates the soldiers' esteem, proclaiming that "[s]he feels that a soldier has a soul to be saved."[8] Nightingale's description of a regiment in Balaclava mustering to return to duty in the trenches shows that the respect was mutual: "From those trenches 30 will never return. Yet they volunteer, press forward for the trenches. . . . And fancy, thro' all this, the army preserving their courage & patience—as they have done. . . . There was something sublime in the spectacle. The brave 39th, whose Regimental Hospitals are the best I have ever seen, turned out & gave Florence Nightingale three times three, as I rode away. There was nothing empty in that cheer or in the heart which received it. I took it as a true expression of true sympathy" (*Duty*, 130).

For the British public, Nightingale and her nurses were models of female heroism, but for the military, they were interlopers whose presence indicated an admission of administrative failure. Compelled by the public's demands to improve hospital conditions, the government created great fanfare when it sent 38 nurses abroad. The government faced a much tougher battle with the entrenched military bureaucracy that had ignored those deplorable conditions. As the superintendent of nurses, Nightingale was seen by many military doctors and bureaucrats as a meddling amateur empowered by her well-placed friends. Private funds, some collected by the *Times*, were put at her disposal, allowing her to circumvent channels and to provide hospitals with needed provisions. The common soldiers were grateful, but officers complained that "Miss Nightingale queens it with absolute power; all the authorities being afraid of the newspapers."[9] At the very least, doctors "reserved for themselves alone the right to judge and criticize the work of the Medical Department," and the superintendent of nurses' observations held no authority.[10] Nightingale described to Liz Herbert a squabble that arose when the nurses' kitchen temporarily interrupted the officers' supply of toast. The angry officers' real grievance, she said, was with the nurses' independence—"we have no prospects to injure. . . . Although subordinate to these Medical Chiefs in office, we are superior to them in influence & in the chance of being heard at home. It is an anomalous position" (*Duty*, 179). This "independence," combined with Nightingale's close ties to Sidney Herbert, ensured that the nurses who arrived to serve in Turkey were viewed with caution by the embattled Horse Guards. Parliament member August Stafford articulated the nurses' threat to the military's authority when he returned from Turkey saying that he had met only two men in the East: Turkish commander Omar Pacha and Florence Nightingale (*Life*, 1:231).

Despite the hagiographic Victorian accounts of the motherly "Santa Filomena," Nightingale's mission was not entirely successful, and her nurses testified that she was far from saintly. Many of her charges were mystified by the discipline she required, strict rules intended to place women above the reproach of doctors ready to fault the new nurses' shortcomings. Misunderstandings arose from the class difference between nurses who worked for wages and their benefactress, leading to complaints such as one in December 1854 that "wee are all so very unappey Miss Nightingale have sum spite against us but for wat cawse wee know not."[11] Nightingale could dismiss nurses' complaints with impatience and insensitivity, while needlessly antagonizing doctors.[12] Similarly, Catholic nuns were alienated by Nightingale's attempts to maintain a secular establishment.[13]

"Three Months from This Day I Publish My Experience": The Creation of Nightingale's *Notes*

Critics have increasingly explored the complexity of Nightingale's position and her work in the Crimean War, but the most revealing account of her administrative genius and skill as a propagandist remains virtually unread. *Notes on Matters Affecting the Health, Efficiency, and Hospital Administration of the British Army* (1858) combines the tenderness of "a Lady with a Lamp" with Wellingtonian fervor and pugnacity; indeed, she approvingly quotes the Duke's letter to an officer that declares, "I wish I had it in my power to give you well-clothed Troops, or to hang those who ought to have given them clothing" (*Notes*, 1:7). The result of her efforts is not merely a polemic on military reform but a passionate elegy for the ordinary British soldier. This enormous collation of fact, official correspondence, and first-person account is little known, anonymity that occurs by Nightingale's own design. She wrote specifically to pressure the government into investigating military hospitals; if her plan worked, the public would never see *Notes*.

After her return from the Crimea, Nightingale was driven to correct the abuses she had seen there. The Roebuck Commission had sent mercilessly accurate reports from Scutari hospital, but government reports ordinarily did not attract a large readership. Without meaningful administrative reform, Nightingale feared that the Crimea tragedy would repeat itself. Her goal, then, was to form a royal commission that would study the workings of the army and bring about fundamental revision of its administration. Nightingale gained the Queen's consent for such an investigation, but she still required the active support of a reluctant Lord Panmure, the secretary of state for war, to carry it out. In October 1856 she was able to extract from Panmure an official request for her experience of the war. Although Panmure asked for her accounting, he did not pledge to act on the abuses she revealed. The secretary anticipated the battles that a royal commission would raise with the War Office, and he avoided the conflict simply by procrastinating.

Nightingale saw Panmure's delay as nothing less than a betrayal, and she forced his hand with *Notes*, a text she wrote in only six months. Panmure may have anticipated that Nightingale would produce a touching wartime memoir. Instead she created a huge annotated text, one that she knew would become a best-seller on the strength of her national popularity. Her scathing evidence and accusation of prominent officials appeared under Panmure's express solicitation of "observation, during the late War, [that] must have furnished you with much important information." In February 1857 she conveyed to Herbert the threat that "three months from this day I publish my experience of the Crimea Campaign and my suggestions for improvement, unless there has been a fair and tangible pledge by that time for reform" (*Florence*, 194).

Nightingale never published her report, critics dryly note, because "the practical reforms she advocated were carried out by the Commission, without recourse to popular agitation."[14] To resort to "agitation," Nightingale knew, risked embarrassing officials at the War Office and ensuring that they would become even more resentful and resistant to change; the royal commission provided the most expedient means to her end. This success meant that only a few copies of *Notes*, printed at Nightingale's expense, were circulated among friends. Its findings were presented to the public under the royal commission's official rubric, just as she had planned. "The War Office itself did not print her Report," her biographer observes, "and thus it never became generally known how much of the report of the subsequent Royal Commission, and how many of the administrative reforms consequent upon it, were in fact the work of Miss Nightingale" (*Life,* 1:343). The combination of statistical brilliance and inflammatory fact had been her insurance policy; when her strategy worked, she buried it.

In its collection of facts, evidence, and correspondence, *Notes* claims to present "the whole history of the frightful Scutari calamity."[15] Like a lawyer arguing a case, Nightingale uses dispassionate statistics to reveal a preventable loss of life, and she allows medical officers to incriminate themselves through their own correspondence. She traces responsibility for the army's disaster to the top of the medical hierarchy, specifically to Dr. John Hall, the chief of medical staff of the British Expeditionary Army. She mercilessly reveals the feeble attempts of Dr. Andrew Smith, director of Army Medical Service, to shore up his department's reputation. In reviewing Smith's correspondence with Dr. John Hall, Nightingale observes:

> One would think that the fact, well known by this time, of an Army having all but perished, would have been of itself a sufficient reason for the severest animadversion from the Head of the Army Medical Department. But no! . . . Dr. Smith writes to his Principal Medical Officer, 'I beg you to supply me, and that immediately,'—with what?—'with every kind of information which you may deem likely to enable me to establish a character for it' (the department), 'which the public appears desirous to prove that it does not possess.' What hope for the Army after this? He might as well have said, Never mind anything if you only enable me to free the Department from blame. (1:xxii)

Nightingale's mockery of the Army Medical Office illustrates that she had no intention of creating a dry government Blue Book. If, despite her efforts, no administrative reforms were forthcoming, her text was designed to cue a large reading public to draw unmistakable conclusions about official incompetence. Only rarely does *Notes* include a first-person account of the miseries that Nightingale witnessed, but those occasional anecdotes were just the details that the public desired. When Nightingale cites a doctor's description of treating barefoot soldiers in midwinter, she corroborates his statement by saying, "I have seen cases so frost-bitten up to the knee" (1:xliii). Such simple, devastating details delivered by an unimpeachable source would have conveyed to readers the horror of the conditions that laid waste to the British army. The combination of reliable data and unforgiving, inflammatory criticism from a national heroine no doubt would have roused public opinion to a fever pitch.

"Oh My Poor Men": Nightingale's Crimean Account

In *Notes on . . . the British Army*, Nightingale solves a mystery, explaining how a tragedy occurred by systematically examining instances in which administrators could have acted to improve conditions. She then substantiates her claims by citing official correspondence and reports, as well as experts' opinions. In this manner, Nightingale comprehensively addresses the points of administrative failure. Factors as different as the inadequate state of laundry service, transport ships, hospital diet, and medical officers' education contributed to a situation that allowed 16,000 men to die of preventable diseases. No detail is too small for Nightingale's consideration, and in explaining the inconsistency of medical statistics, she critiques even the forms used in military hospitals. As she reviews evidence of medical incompetence from early in the war, she observes that "it reminds one of the prologue in an ancient drama, dimly shadowing forth the crime to be evolved in the play and the retribution which is to follow" (*Notes,* 1:vii). The level of neglect that she witnessed is criminal. The effect of such carelessness is nothing short of murder. Examining data on engineering, sanitation, architecture, and nutrition, she calculates the number of soldiers in the Home Army who died needlessly from disease. By following the recommendations she had gathered, "we should save nearly 1,500 good soldiers yearly, who, from all experiences in all other cases, are as certainly killed by the neglects specified as if they were drawn up on Salisbury Plain and shot" (*Notes,* 504).

Nightingale's text ridicules the medical department's most offensive blunders, but derision alone could not prove the need for hospital reform. Her combination of sarcasm, analysis, and passion is a singular one. "There is nothing like figures to be impressive," she writes Sidney Herbert from the Crimea. Details were damning, and she supplies them in abundance. For example, in February 1855 she reports that the purveyor's storeroom contained one mop, three flannel shirts, and one package of needles for the 3,600 men in Scutari Barracks Hospital (*Duty*, 83–85). Added to this appreciation for "figures" is Nightingale's drive to vindicate the sufferings she had witnessed. A private note from 1856 shows her haunted by the army's lost men: "Oh my poor men who endured so patiently. I feel I have been such a bad mother to you to come home & leave you lying in your Crimean grave. 73 per cent in eight regiments during six months from disease alone—but who thinks of that now? If I could carry any one point which would prevent any part of the recurrence of this our colossal calamity . . . then I should have been true to the cause of those brave dead" (*Ever Yours*, 171). The Crimean dead are both tragic casualties and appalling statistics, and even Nightingale's expression of grief bristles with authoritative facts. For Nightingale, figures are the most accurate, concise method of describing her military hospital experience. In *Notes*, she works to ensure that statistics testify to tragedy without dehumanizing the suffering she witnessed. When she estimates that 58,000 British troops died from preventable causes over the course of 15 years, Nightingale reminds readers that "these are figures on the page—but, to us, these figures are men" (*Notes*, 10:vii).

The previous chapter documented the manner in which *Suggestions for Thought* linked empirical observation and religious truth. Similarly, *Notes on . . . the British Army* proposes using the facts of the Scutari disaster to reveal a larger principle about sanitation and hospital operation. Nightingale saw the army's enormous loss and subsequent recovery from disease as a test case, one that could "point out a great and invariable law of nature" that must be heeded to maintain the health of the army (*Notes*, 561). Toward this end, her recounting of her Crimea experience opens with a collection of indisputable statistics. In the siege of Sebastopol, seven times more men died from disease than from wounds. The percentage varied by regiment: those regiments that treated their men in the field lost fewer than those whose troops were shipped from Sebastapol to the hospitals in Turkey, where a cholera epidemic raged. Restating the case, she says that "10,053 men, or 60 per cent. per annum, perished in seven months, from disease alone, upon an average strength of 28,939. This mortality exceeds that of the Great Plague" (7, 12B).

Statistics tell a story, or as Nightingale argues, a "truth" about their circumstances. That truth depends upon statistical accuracy, and she finds wartime accounting to be slipshod at best; as she tries to establish the army's mortality rate, she finds that "I have carefully compared the statistics from six different official sources and none of them agree" (*Notes*, 309). For example, the chief medical officer's record for the last quarter of 1854 shows 400 fewer deaths than the adjutant's listing of burials. The discrepancy, she claims, probably underestimates army deaths; more significantly, it damages medical officers' credibility. "However satisfactory they may be to the departments who have put them forth . . . [such records] convey no trustworthy idea as to the sickness and mortality of the army in the East, and that, for any practical purpose, they are put forth to the public, who are most interested in the matter, not absolute truths, but only approximations" (311).

With this qualification, Nightingale carefully documents data taken from "official and authentic sources" and explains the methodology used to arrive at her figures (*Notes*, 10:i). She also illustrates how medical officers manipulate statistics to downplay hospital casualties. Dr. John Hall was a master of the medical bureaucracy who had hoped for a more prestigious position than the post he received in the Crimea. He resented Nightingale's arrival with her nurses, and she was infuriated with his negligence. On 20 October 1854 Hall wrote to Dr. Andrew Smith in London, claiming that the Scutari hospitals had "now been put on a very creditable footing and that nothing is lacking" (*Florence,* 145). Hall's official opinion never changed, even while a cholera epidemic raged during the dismal winter of 1854 to 1855.

Nightingale's analysis of Hall's report is withering. *Notes* quotes Dr. Hall's claims that "[s]ickness has been very much diminished and so has Mortality. In January last [1855] the number of deaths was 1,480, in February, 1,254, and in March, 424, every month showing a steady decrease over the preceding one. The average mortality, at present, is 5 1/7 per diem." Nightingale argues that "[t]his problem is much like the celebrated riddle, 'Given the height of the mast, to tell the captain's name.' *Not* given the numbers in Hospital, to tell whether there is a 'steady decrease' in its mortality" (*Notes*, 3:xxx). At best, she observes, the doctor's statement is conveniently incomplete. "A 'mortality of 5 1/7 per diem' does not sound alarming, certainly, but it is 1,877 per *annum*." Furthermore, the information Hall provides is useless without knowing the total number of patients. Nightingale reasons that "1,877 Deaths on a strength of 8,000 sick, which there was at one time, being a very different thing from 1,877 Deaths on a strength of 3,000 sick, which there was at another time" (3:xxx–xxxi).

Nightingale's scrutiny of Dr. Hall's correspondence documents medical officials' use of convenient accounting to avoid alarming their superiors. She cites Hall's letter of April 1855 to Lord Raglan, leader of the British expeditionary forces, which finds that "the general health of the Army continues steadily to improve. . . . During the present week the admissions to strength have been in the ratio of 3.93 per cent, and the deaths to strength of 0.38 per cent" (*Notes*, 293). Medical reports are intended to advise army commanders of the strength of their forces, Nightingale reasons, and such disingenuous reporting "is simply misleading to the authorities, unless indeed, which is hardly likely, they are thoroughly *au fait* of statistical inquiries." With meticulous detail, *Notes* explains the ramifications of the numbers provided by the chief medical officer:

> 0.52, 3.93 per cent look nothing.
> But multiply 3.9 by 52=2,028, in order to find the annual admissions per 1,000; and it will be seen that the whole force will go twice through hospital in a year, at that rate. And multiply 14.3 [the admissions rate for March 1855] by 52=7,436 per 1,000 per annum; and the whole force will go seven times through hospital in a year. . . . Multiply [the death rate of] 0.52 by 52 in the same way, and it will be found that . . . more than one-fourth of the whole population of the army will perish in a year. (293–294)

The figures obscured by medical officials told a chilling story, one that Nightingale sought to make readily accessible to her potential readers. To ensure that the public immediately recognized the significance of the army's mortality statistics, Nightingale developed an innovative pie chart to compare military and civilian mortality. The army's monthly deaths are represented by proportionately sized wedges. At a glance, the sliver representing a mortality of 8.4 per thousand at the beginning of the war contrasts sharply with the bulging triangle of January 1855: a rate of 1,173.6 per thousand. A small circle at the center of these wedges represents mortality in Manchester; at 12.4 per thousand a year, this industrial city was one of the most unhealthy in England. Nightingale's chart shows clearly the progress of disease among the troops, as well as the army's recovery to a mortality rate lower than that of Manchester's. As a "flank march upon the enemy," she sent framed copies to the Horse Guards, the War Office, and the Army Medical Department (Smith, 88).

Early in her tenure in the East, Nightingale wrote Herbert, "It is a sad joke here that a large reward has been offered for any one who is personally responsible, barring the Commandant" (*Ever Yours,* 89). Her strategy of citing medical officials' correspondence, made available by the royal commission, unveils the mysteries of official responsibility. By patiently tracing officials' response to particular events, she lays blame squarely upon the Army Medical Service, specifically upon Dr. Hall. Hall hardly could have been oblivious to a calamitous mortality rate and abysmal sanitary conditions that, Nightingale archly notes, were "obvious to any one with a nose" (*Notes,* 3:viii). The principal medical officer had claimed that "nothing is lacking" at the Scutari hospitals, and he defended his assessment by denying or ignoring evidence to the contrary. As Herbert wrote to Lord Raglan, "I cannot help feeling that Dr. Hall resents offers of assistance as being slurs on his preparations" (*Life,* 1:288). Even the field marshal failed in attempts to make the army's hospitals accountable. With little effect, Raglan rebuked Hall's administration in the army's general orders, saying that "the Commander of the Forces is very sorry to have to animadvert very strongly upon the conduct of the medical department" (*Raglan,* 214).

Nightingale's relentless case against Hall is best illustrated by her lengthy "history" of the doctor's search for lime juice. *Notes* cites army memoranda to document that, by November 1854, salt rations, insufficient clothes and blankets, and inadequate attention to sanitation contributed to widespread incidence of scurvy. Rather than address the systemic problems that left fewer soldiers in the trenches than in the hospitals, senior doctors focused their attention on a simplistic remedy: limes. *Notes* includes numerous letters between November 1854 and January 1855 in which Hall and Smith confirm the pounds of limes ordered and the estimated arrival dates. She then reviews the result of their meticulous shipping catalogue—their sole plan for treating scurvy:

> The history of this Lime Juice, which is now brought to a conclusion, is so painfully instructive, that it must here be summed up.
>
> The "Esk" had arrived with the Lime Juice on December 10 [1854], and though there is some controversy about the date within a few days, she had, at all events, landed her cargo by December 20. This is nowhere denied.
>
> Dr. Hall had been advised in time by Dr. Smith both of her day of sailing, her name, her cargo, and even the name of its consignee, the Commissary-General, as also that the Lime Juice was for the use of the Troops.

Yet it appears to have remained for Lord Raglan to discover its existence on January 24 (six weeks after it was so grievously needed by an
Army melting away from Scurvy), through his Order to the Commissary-
General to send him returns of everything in store. . . . It appears to have
been left to Lord Raglan's own detective power to be here his own Sanitary Officer. (*Notes*, 1:xvii)

Nightingale presents the appalling facts of the deadly winter of 1854
to 1855 in addition to letters documenting the indifference of the most
senior medical officers. In January 1855 after three months without
vegetables, almost 8,000 patients were being treated for disease, primarily dysentery and diarrhea. Of those patients, 2,253 died. Dr. Hall's
assessment, dated 11 January 1855, is that "[s]ymptoms of Scurvy have
made their appearance in some cases; but as yet the disease has not
made much progress amongst the men . . . and I hope by the arrival of
the expected supply of Lime Juice, its further spread will be prevented"
(*Notes*, 1:xiv). *Notes* highlights the inaccuracies of Hall's correspondence,
underscoring the effect of the medical service's administrative neglect:
"The expression 'symptoms of Scurvy' seems quite inexplicable, as well
as that of its 'not having made much progress.' The Army was dying,
and of Scurvy. More than half the Infantry was sick in Hospital during
this month; and the mortality was 1,173 per annum. . . . Yet there is
nothing to indicate in these letters that either Principal Medical Officer
or Director-General know, that an Army is dying, or that it is any business of theirs" (1:xiv–xv).

From its critique of individual medical officers, *Notes* draws larger
conclusions about the system that allowed such conduct. The regimental organization provided doctors little opportunity to confer with their
colleagues; consequently, military hospitals offered fewer opportunities
for research than civilian hospitals. Competent physicians were promoted into administrative posts for which they had no experience. The
system's "radical defect," of course, was its glaring lack of accountability.
Notes observes that "the administrative principle of the Horse Guards is
an admirable plan for shifting all responsibility till it is not known where
it lies. If you treat your Director General like a school-boy, you will have
a school-boy for your Director General" (*Notes*, 1:xxv). In place of this
haphazard arrangement, Nightingale suggests new methods for delivering supplies, standardizing army hygiene, and establishing lines of
authority. Her recommendations are sweeping but also clear and practical. Smith observes that Nightingale created nothing less than a "self-

acting, self-regulating system, embodying individual will-power in action, designed to secure the maximum output of useful work for the total money and manpower expended" (*Reputation,* 81).

Notes compiles a comprehensive list of administrative defects followed by an equally comprehensive list of solutions. Instructions are given for more efficiently incorporating sanitation into army decisions. A section on diet provides expert knowledge on nutrition and includes recipes such as "Cheap Plain Rice Pudding for Campaigning." "The 'Regulations' Book is very clever," Nightingale observes, "but it is no cook" (*Notes,* 14:xx). *Notes* addresses even the management of hospital orderlies, observing that all male and female nurses should be able to read. In addition, it tersely notes that "if attendants cannot be trained to keep the rooms ventilated without draughts, there is a defect of intelligence in the particular individuals, and attendance on the sick is not their calling" (489).

In contrast to its focus on sanitation and unambiguous administration, *Notes* offers surprisingly few descriptions of actual nursing. The superintendent of nurses illustrates her charges' work with general maxims, such as instructions for moving the sick and wounded. Nightingale advises that "[c]holera can best be treated where the man is attacked. Lay the man down, if possible, then and there in blankets, and treat him there. . . . In wounds, there are always 24 hours' respite, before inflammatory symptoms set in, when it does the wounded no harm to be moved" (*Notes,* 198).

Discussions of Nightingale's novel nursing establishment most often arise as *Notes* clarifies the nurses' mission and defends itself against criticism. Dr. Smith's description of the Scutari hospitals' hygiene is one example of how authorities downplayed the nurses' contributions. *Notes* cites Smith's testimony of March 1855, which speaks generally to the inappropriate presence of women in a military theater. He contrasts feminine, domestic standards with masculine, wartime standards, observing that "I was perfectly aware that females can see many things, in which there might be a deficiency of cleanliness and comfort, that men do not see, and even that men have not time to see; because the medical officers were overwhelmed with work—there might be a spot upon a sheet that a medical officer would not notice, and a woman would at once" (*Notes,* 98). *Notes* uses analytical evidence to counter Smith's depiction of feminine impracticality, including doctors' reports that hospital linen was usually filthy or infested with lice. Because contractors often neglected to boil the laundry, clothing and linen could be

returned to patients with vermin intact. Nightingale's charts conveniently illustrate the amount and type of laundry processed, and her
inventory calculates that only 2 1/4 items per man were washed during
January 1855. Smith's attempts to dismiss nurses' squeamishness are
fruitless against the fact that during one month hospitals could provide
only 132 clean towels for 2,400 patients. Nightingale uses Smith's analogy to summarize hospitals' neglect, observing, "Had not the matter
been too destructive of life, health, morality, and discipline, to be fit
subject for a joke, one would be tempted to think that one authority at
least had been in jest when he said that the use of the Female Nurses
going out was to see 'a spot upon a sheet.' At that time, sheets were not,
at least such as could be used" (109).

Correspondence from doctors reveals that they blamed the army hospitals' poor publicity on the party of 38 women and philanthropists such
as the superintendent of nurses. In this climate, nurses became scape-
goats for a host of minor accusations. The most petty, perhaps, is the
example of a raw mutton chop that inconveniently appeared on a
patient's plate during inspection. The chop raised an inquiry into hospital cooking conditions and was eventually discussed in the Roebuck
investigation. *Notes* cites a beleaguered doctor's testimony that "the
kitchen had been occupied by Miss Nightingale a great deal, so that the
Hospital cooks had not an opportunity of cooking the patients' dinners
properly" (*Notes*, 363). Nightingale indignantly defends herself, citing
the cook's evidence that "Miss Nightingale and her Nurses never set
foot in the General Kitchen." From the Crimea, Nightingale privately
complained that "Dr. Hall does not think it beneath him to . . . give out
that we are private adventurers & to be treated as such" (*Ever Yours*,
133). Sidney Herbert accused her of paranoia and chastised her for writing letters about her critics that showed "an irritation and a vehemence
which detracts very much from about the weight [which would] otherwise attach to what you say" (*Duty*, 218). Nightingale pondered his
scolding and worried, "Have I injured the work by showing 'vehemence
or irritation'[?]" Her reply to Herbert, though, is typically concise and
confident: "I thought & considered. And I determined I had not. I think
I can prove my assertion" (245).

Nightingale conducted her experiment with female nurses in an
atmosphere of distrust and suspicion, and those tensions are reflected in
Notes' emphasis on the discipline and morality of nurses. Although
Nightingale sought to improve their training and competence, she
points to the deportment of nurses as the key to the success of the pro-

fession. "[I]t is absolutely necessary," she claims, "that the high character and respectability of the female must be maintained, both as to her
personal and official conduct; and no motives of supposed utility should
be allowed to require or lead her to do that which would lower her
morally or officially" (*Notes*, 167). The report fails to mention the Scutari
nurses who were dismissed for drinking or who abandoned their duties
to marry soldiers. Neither does it refer to the rebellious nurses who
grumbled about the unflattering uniforms: Nightingale's letters record
a Mrs. Lawfield who complained, "[I]f I'd known, Ma'am about the
Caps . . . I wouldn't have come, Ma'am" (*Ever Yours*, 83). The text
alludes to these disappointments only by saying that "those who showed
themselves inefficient, or became so, were dismissed upon individual
grounds" (*Notes*, 160). These disciplinary struggles underlie Nightingale's caution about nurses mingling during off-duty hours: "[I]t must
be considered that association in large dormitories tends to corrupt the
good and make the bad worse" (487).

Notes is a partisan history designed to convince an audience of the
legitimacy of female nursing and of the need for extensive army hospital
reform. The nursing establishment portrayed in *Notes* is "entirely subor-
dinated to the medical authority" (*Notes*, 159). Furthermore, Nightingale's text opens with a properly feminine disclaimer. Nightingale anticipates criticism that "such matters are beyond my sphere" by citing her
official authorization and by declaring that her observations address a
general need, not just a limited, military one (*Notes*, Preface, 1). Within
this properly subordinate position, though, Nightingale makes claims
for elevating the professional status of nurses above the level of char-
women. They "should not be charged with the mere drudgery in the
necessary cleansing and labour of a Military Hospital, but should be
made capable of performing what may be termed 'skilled' nursing, by a
course of previous instruction" (*Notes*, 159). Nightingale's nursing project employs domestic authority, an authority derived from "the morality that maternal instinct was assumed to bestow on all women."[16] This
domestic authority allowed Nightingale to dismiss Smith's "spot upon a
sheet" characterization of gender roles; it also led her to imagine an ide-
alized, harmonious hospital climate arising from the combination of
innate masculine chivalry and feminine virtue. Nurses, she claims, exert
"a moral influence which has now been proved, beyond all doubt, to be
highly beneficial to the soldier" (*Notes*, 159). Nightingale's anecdotes
assert that the moral benefits arise from the mere presence of women,
and her sentimental descriptions of British enlisted men contrast sharply

with her scathing denunciations of medical officers: "Tears come into my eyes as I think how, amidst scenes of horrible filth, of loathsome disease and death, there rose above it all the innate dignity, gentleness, and chivalry of the men . . . shining in the midst of what must be considered as the lowest sinks of human misery, and preventing instinctively the use of one expression which could distress a gentlewoman" (94).

Citing women's moral authority and the respect that men grant it, *Notes* claims the patients' bedsides for Nightingale's nurses, arguing that the duties most directly affecting soldiers can be best performed or supervised by women. Nightingale illustrates her case with the example of patients' "close-stools." Medical officers and sanitary commissioners had directed orderlies to empty the patients' chamber pots regularly, but military orders could not compel the orderlies to remove the offensive objects more than once each day. *Notes* suggests that men are not suited to perform such essentially domestic, female work: "And is it fair to ask Medical Officers, to see to these details of drudgery? My own belief, founded on much experience, is, that it can only be effectually done by a woman; it is done in the Civil Hospitals by her; it has been done in Military ones by her. . . . [F]or my sake they [orderlies] performed offices of this kind (which they neither would for the sake of discipline, nor for that of the importance of their own health, which they did not know), and never one word nor one look which a gentleman would not have used" (*Notes*, 93–94).

Notes observes that a siege is fought by two armies: One in combat with the enemy and one in combat with disease. The army had failed miserably at the essentially domestic duties that prevented disease, and Nightingale reappropriated those tasks for her nurses: Laundering clothes, keeping patients bathed and fed, and maintaining an orderly hospital staff. Nightingale implies that women have more aptitude than men in these departments; in a less threatening manner, she also depicts nurses as allowing doctors to function more efficiently. Neither medical officers nor ward masters can best maintain hospital discipline, a task much like a middle-class woman instructing her household's servants. Ward masters should "enforce every rule except that which pertains to the bedside of the patient; this last can only be done by women, not with their own hands, but by directing and training orderlies; it is an humble prerogative which no one will grudge them" (*Notes*, 94).

Nightingale carefully argues for the introduction of female nursing, but she also lays the groundwork for support of hospital reform. She invites public indignation by comparing the army's standards to "the same state of the Soldiery . . . which Shakespeare and Froissart describe as existing in the British Army before the battle of Agincourt, and before those of Cressy and Poitiers" (*Notes*, 262). Appeals to the public's hearts are accompanied by appeals to their pocketbooks: Readers are reminded that repairing buildings is cheaper than replacing men. She builds her argument objectively by reporting that the country spends up to £120 per year for every trained soldier that dies in service abroad; furthermore, *Notes* observes the inefficiency of having 12,025 men in the hospital and only 11,367 available for duty (230, 235). The events of the Scutari hospitals reveal a "truth" or "law" about nature and the army's health, Nightingale argues, knowledge that could save lives at every army outpost. Colonial expansion into tropical climates made attending to this "truth" even more important: "The British race has carried with it into those regions of the sun its habits, its customs, and its vices, without considering that there are penalties exacted by nature in her tropical dominions from those who neglect or transgress her laws far more severe than in the more temperate climates of our own country" (565).

Events affecting the army in "those regions of the sun" allowed Nightingale to make an additional appeal to British chauvinism. Her text was written in the wake of the Indian Mutiny of 1857, the sepoy uprising that left the Queen's subjects horrified by tales of Europeans killed by Indian troops in Meerut and Cawnpore. With the knowledge that additional soldiers would be sent to the Indian subcontinent, Nightingale sells her reforms by playing on national pride, making sweeping claims for the Anglo-Saxon character and the British imperial mission. She recasts a poorly conceived, ill-executed war over Russian influence in Constantinople as a noble event of epic proportions, one in which "the Anglo-Saxon on the Crimean heights has won for himself a greater name than the Spartan at Thermopylae, as the six months' struggle to endure was a greater proof of what man can do, than the six hours' struggle to fight" (*Notes*, 508). Since sepoys could no longer be depended upon to guard British territories, Nightingale argued that the empire was threatened by the inadequate organization and unsanitary conditions of army hospitals. If a tiny island were to control the Indian colony, its human resources must be conserved: "The time appears to have arrived, when by the British race alone must the integrity of that Empire be upheld. The conquering race must retain possession. And experience has shown that, without special information and skillful application of the resources of science in preserving health, the drain upon our home population must exhaust our means" (518).

The interests of empire depend upon healthy soldiers, and Nightingale argues that the Crimean experience proves that soldiers' health is improved by female nurses. Nurses serve their country's soldiers and, by extension, make possible the soldiers' expansion into inhospitable climates. Nightingale asserts that whereas hygiene can become "the handmaid of civilization," sharing European scientific knowledge with the rest of the world, nurses can become imperialism's true handmaids by serving their country's soldiers abroad (*Notes*, 567). By introducing nurses into the debate on the British policy in India, Nightingale looked to the future of military nursing, working to ensure that her experiment would not end with the employment of 38 women in the Crimea. In an attempt to appeal to the public's jingoistic sensibilities, *Notes* even employs observations of British racial superiority, while carefully excepting the German House of Hanover: The army is composed of "only the finest specimens of the finest physical race in the world, with the exception, perhaps, of some part of our aristocracy" (494).

Surprisingly, Nightingale's text also attempts to revise the stereotype of the working-class enlisted man. In its most punitive form, bias against the working class allowed officers to implicate soldiers for their own sickness. Nightingale cites a letter from Dr. Alexander Cumming, a member of the Commission of Enquiry sent to Crimea in 1854, which blames patients for the breakdown of sanitation. Cumming's report to Dr. Smith finds that "the unsatisfactory state of the privies has been noticed by all, but no means have yet been found altogether to amend it. It is entirely, or nearly so, attributable to the careless dirty habits of the patients themselves; suggestions on this point were made by the Civil Engineer who accompanies the Sanitary Commissioners" (*Notes*, 3:xiv). As part of her plan to offer patients alternatives to drinking and gambling, Nightingale provided the "careless dirty" soldier with educational lectures, the chance to remit money home to his family, and a coffeehouse named for the battle of Inkerman. A reading room in the Barrack Hospital provided men a place to write letters and read newspapers; although officers had predicted that soldiers would sell the papers for liquor, Nightingale declared that "the Library of the British Museum could not have presented a more silent or orderly scene" (454–55). *Notes* argues that the soldiers' environment shapes their behavior, and it chides doctors who neglect the health of their working-class patients, faulting the pseudoscience of a medical text, "On the Feigned Diseases of Soldiers and Sailors": "Like Sir Walter Scott's 'Demonology and Witchcraft,' this book was written on the principle of raking up all the wonders of a past and credulous age, in modern and agreeable language, instead of the original Black-Letter Annals of King James. . . . As modern Science and attentive humanity have driven witchcraft from the tribunals of our country, so must the improvement in science, good feeling and caution of the Medical Officers dispel that unreasoning belief in malingering which once pervaded the Service" (366).

As she emphasizes the army's need for medical reform, Nightingale serves as an envoy bringing news of the common soldier to the upper class. She advises her peers of subtle changes in class status that ensure the soldier cannot be so easily manipulated; she cautions, "It must not forgotten that the intelligence of these working classes has undergone a great advance of late years, and that the details of the Crimean catastrophe as well as the neglects from which it arose are perfectly well known among them" (*Notes*, 509). Officers, who brought their own servants to the battlefield, could have little idea of the enlisted men's situation or of their suffering.[17] The conventional wisdom of the army's officers, she says, is that "there are three causes which make a soldier enlist, viz., being out of work, in a state of intoxication, or jilted by his sweetheart. Yet the incentives to enlistment, which we desire to multiply, can hardly be put by Englishmen of the nineteenth century, in this form, viz., more poverty, more drink, more faithless sweethearts" (65–66). The army can scarcely hope to attract a "better class" of soldier with only these negative "incentives," she says, and the specter of disease could make it altogether impossible, "as civilisation advances," for the army to sign up enough recruits for the colonies (65). Nightingale even poses the possibility that, in the future, the common soldier could rebel at outrageous treatment such as that he received in Crimea. From a "competent authority," she offers the prospect of mutiny: "[The] men are not in a mood to be trifled with. They are in that sort of savage frame of mind which would delight in tearing somebody to pieces—they would prefer a Brahmin, or a Musselman, but as they cannot get that, they would take what they could get. If Cholera should break out badly in our Barracks, and should be traced to the neglect of timely and repeated warnings, it would fare ill with the responsible" (519).

With threat and flattery, hard science and merciless bullying, *Notes* make its case for fundamental administrative change in military hospitals. It recounts Nightingale's experience in the Crimea through correspondence, official reports, and statistical analysis, a strategy that provides the most chilling yet credible details of cholera symptoms and sanitation abuses. Her tribute to the army's dead, alternately consisting

of righteous anger and cold, dispassionate fury, clearly reveals the effects
of Nightingale's Crimean experiment. "Upon those who watched, week
after week and month after month, this enduring courage, this unalter-
able patience, simplicity, and good sense, this voiceless strength to suffer
and 'be still,' it has made an impression never to be forgotten" (*Notes*,
507). The scenes she witnessed, her biographer claimed, remained her
most vivid recollections: "In extreme old age, when failing powers were
not equally alert to every call, she would sometimes, I have been told,
show listlessness if her companion talked of nurses or nursing, but the
old light would ever come into her eye, and the faltering mind would
instantly stand at attention, upon the slightest reference to the British
soldier" (*Life*, 1:282). *Notes* honors the Crimean soldier by recording his
plight and pledging to improve conditions for his comrades. Nightingale's mission to reform hospitals, fueled by the memories of her "poor
men," would guide the rest of her long career.

Chapter Five

Nightingale as Administrator: Writings on Nursing and India

In *Notes on Matters Affecting the Health, Efficiency, and Hospital Administration of the British Army* (1858), Nightingale relates her experience of the Crimean War and memorializes the victims of administrative incompetence. Perhaps the most remarkable aspect of her virtuoso melding of statistics, expert opinion, and righteous anger is that her 800-page monograph is only one of the many equally complex projects she conducted simultaneously. After her return from the Crimea in 1856, Nightingale became a de facto cabinet member, advising Sidney Herbert, now secretary for war, and a circle of sanitary and medical experts who lobbied for health reforms. Public policy regarding the health of the British army was shaped in her rooms in the Burlington Hotel, quarters that the reformers called "the Little War Office." Nightingale described her collaboration with Herbert as "exactly like two men—exactly like him and Gladstone" (*Ever Yours,* 231). She focused the reformers' efforts, gathering information and interpreting it for the public officials who could help enact the required legislation. Meanwhile, she continued to publish articles on a variety of issues related to nursing, including topics such as developing nursing schools, improving hospital design, and extending health care to the poor. Nightingale considered herself to be "in office" until 1872, while political allies such as Lord Palmerston, the prime minister, and Lord de Grey, the secretary for war, were in power. From the time of her return from the Crimea until her "retirement," her publishing was prodigious.

Nightingale's chronic poor health after her return from the Crimea makes the range and detail of her work even more surprising. Her labors for the Sanitary Commission were tireless during the summer of 1857. The uninvited company of her mother and sister, though, complicated her work. Old family tensions resurfaced when Fanny and Parthe moved to the Burlington and brought their distracting social duties to Nightingale's rooms. She claimed that the pair, observing her relentless schedule of meetings and deadlines, told her, "You lead a very amusing life" (*Flo-*

rence, 199). By the end of the summer, Nightingale demanded to be left "alone, quite alone," and on 11 August 1857, she suffered a physical breakdown that left her an invalid (206). Thereafter, Nightingale's physical symptoms and "neurasthenia" rarely allowed her to leave her sofa, and all visitors were screened carefully to avoid exacerbating her inexplicable heart palpitations.

Nightingale treated her condition by rejecting everything but her work. Close friends were told the sick woman could spare no time for visiting, and even the queen of Holland was denied entry. After the onset of this illness, the mere threat of a call from her mother or sister would send Nightingale's pulse racing. The uncertainty of her health added urgency to her demands and drove her to work herself and those around her even harder. One critic observes that "her illness allowed her to do a prodigious amount of work from her invalid couch, and to tyrannise those with whom she worked."[1] Nightingale abandoned her public role as a Lady with a Lamp to live a reclusive, private existence. The choice, she told her friend Mary Mohl, was "entirely the effect of calculation. I cannot live to work unless I give up all that makes life pleasant" (*Ever Yours*, 262). Her friend Benjamin Jowett recognized Nightingale's "calculation" when he observed in 1866, "Sometimes I think that the Doctors ought to cure you: sometimes that you ought to cure yourself" (*Jowett's Letters*, 81).

Nightingale's mysterious malady ensured that she never worked as a nurse after her return from the Crimea. Instead, her illness effectively secured for her the space and privacy needed for the exhaustive task of health care reform. Her research, writing, and political agitation were continual; in 1868, she complained to her father of "men throwing their business upon me which they ought to do themselves" (*Ever Yours*, 296). A letter to Dr. John Sutherland, a sanitarian and fellow reformer, complained melodramatically that "I am so busy I have not time to die" (268).

She focused her unremitting labor on what she called "the work," and the result is a body of writing that shows her broad interpretation of sanitation reform. In meticulously documented government Blue Books and in widely circulated popular journals, Nightingale agitated for the changes she believed would save lives. Improving public health required not just developing schools for nurses but also training nurses to serve where they would be needed most: in rural areas with no access to doctors, in workhouses where convalescent paupers were forced to care for the sick, or with the army stationed abroad. The texts did not offer the most scientific theories of contagion and disease control, and they clearly reflect Nightingale's personal biases. Yet because of her famous deeds in the Crimea, her writings shaped public opinion. Her writing "maintained her reputation, and effectively mapped out the boundaries within which the subject of military nursing could be discussed" (*Angels*, 71). The Nightingale canon includes more than 150 articles and books on subjects ranging from the need for accurate surgical statistics to suggestions for reforming the Poor Law. This chapter examines three texts written after her return from the Crimea that are significant for their scope and style. *Subsidiary Notes as to the Introduction of Female Nursing into Military Hospitals in Peace and in War* (1858) articulates Nightingale's vision of the nursing profession and reveals the difficulties encountered in the Crimea by her pioneering band of nurses. Her most popular text, *Notes on Nursing* (1860), offers insight into the tensions faced by nursing reformers and reveals Nightingale's own experience as an invalid. Her most detailed examination of the British army in India is summarized in *Observations on the Evidence Contained in the Stational Reports* (1863), a book written in her characteristically trenchant style. Indian administrator Sir Bartle Frere claimed that Nightingale's influence in India had grown from this widely read tract, "a certain little red book of hers on India which made some of us very savage at the time, but did us all immense good" (*Bio-Bibliography*, 60).

Nightingale once deflected her mother's criticism by saying that a woman in her unusual position should not be chided or second-guessed. She observed in 1861 that "[n]o woman ever before directed the labours of a Government office. She must be the judge as to the when & the how, if a woman chooses to undertake to direct men over whom she can have no legitimate or recognized control, she shall do it. No one else can judge how she shall do it" (*Ever Yours,* 240). In her zeal to enact meaningful health care reforms, Nightingale's arguments can appear extreme, incomplete, or inconsistent. She instructed viceroys on the importance of sanitation, but she "never grasped the complexities of Indian geography, caste, poverty, and social inertia" (*Reputation,* 148). Her suggestions for maintaining nurses' discipline are at times draconian. The excesses found in Nightingale's texts on nursing and on India offer insight into the "when & the how" of her often awkward position as a civilian, female expert on army hospitals and sanitation. In the spirit and the scope of these texts, we can most clearly see the administrator that Jowett playfully called, "Florence the first, Queen of Nurses[,] Maîtresse of drôlesses[,] Governess of the Governors of India[,] Reverend Mother Superior[,] Mother of the British Army " (*Jowett's Letters,* 153).

"This Coarse, Repulsive, Servile, Noble Work": Subsidiary Notes as to the Introduction of Female Nursing into Military Hospitals in Peace and in War

When Nightingale returned from the Crimea, Lord Panmure, the secretary of state for war, requested her reflections on military nursing administration. The result was a four-page "tentative and experimental" essay that she soon expanded into *Subsidiary Notes*, her treatise on nursing. *Subsidiary Notes* (1858) was published as the second, complementary volume to *Notes on . . . the British Army*, and the pairing is appropriate (*Bio-Bibliography*, 15). Whereas Nightingale's first volume provides statistics and correspondence documenting the Crimean hospitals' failure, *Subsidiary Notes* offers a more personal history of the daily events Nightingale witnessed. The evidence and subject matter of *Notes on . . . the British Army* made it serious, even dismal reading; in contrast, *Subsidiary Notes* offers more domestic details and anecdotes. Elizabeth Gaskell claimed that "[i]t was so interesting I could not leave it." The novelist finished reading the book in a single morning and complimented its advice for cleaning grates, as well as its "quiet continual devout references to God which make the book a holy one" (*Life,* 1:347).

Much of the text that Gaskell so admired was borrowed. Nightingale copied three chapters of her work from Jane Shaw Stewart, a baronet's daughter who served in Balaclava's Castle Hospital during the Crimean War. After the war, Shaw Stewart became the superintendent of nurses at Woolwich General Hospital, introducing nurses to that military institution. Although Nightingale's correspondence refers to Shaw Stewart as a follower of her mission, "she was very much more than this. She was the joint creator, as well as the Superintendent, of the first official corps of female army nurses" (*Angels,* 73). The chapters in *Subsidiary Notes* headed "Hospital Nurses," "Nurses in Civil Hospitals," and "Nurses in Her Majesty's Hospitals," were taken from Shaw Stewart's "Confidential Memorandum"; other chapters on French hospital design also borrow from her correspondence. Nightingale made the text her own by adding several chapters, including information about her service at Scutari, and by phrasing Shaw Stewart's ideas in her own more argumentative style. In addition, she is critical of the Anglican sisterhoods that Shaw Stewart favored. When the original author protested at the treatment of her text, she was told that Nightingale had become too ill to correspond with her (310–11).

The fact that Nightingale took credit for what was, in fact, a collaborative effort, can only increase our appreciation of historians' observations that her "achievements were neither as rapid nor as unqualified as has sometimes been suggested, and that her work was by no means the earliest or the only initiative in the field of British nursing reform" ("Gamp," 366). Her adept political maneuvering also assisted her in gaining publicity for the text. Nightingale frequently fed government documents to the journalist Harriet Martineau in the hopes that she would publicize issues in the popular press. As she passed along *Subsidiary Notes*, Nightingale advised Martineau that "I send it to you only, because there has been so much rant and cant about us [nurses] so much misapprehension about what we do and so much about what we do not do, chiefly by the female ink bottles (in which you are very sure I do not include yourself), that it may interest you to know what a very plain, matter of fact thing Military Hospital Nursing really is" (*Ever Yours,* 203). Nightingale's correspondence with Martineau, the crusading journalist, indicates that Nightingale considered *Subsidiary Notes* part of an effort to counter the effects of critical "ink bottles" and to improve the reputation of female military nurses. Appropriating Shaw Stewart's text was only part of her larger propagandist campaign.

Shaw Stewart's notes were labeled "Confidential Memorandum" in part because female military nurses continued to be a controversial topic; many doctors and officers still objected to their presence at army facilities. Not surprisingly, then, the tone of *Subsidiary Notes* is guarded, rightly so considering the events at the time of the text's conception. Nightingale sent her initial, "tentative" memorandum to Lord Panmure just a week before Woolwich Artillery Hospital removed all but two of its female nurses. In a letter to Panmure, she noted the irony of his order to introduce nurses to military hospitals just as the Army Medical Board turned them out. *Subsidiary Notes* depicts the experimental state of the profession, declaring that the method for achieving hospital nursing "is to a large extent to be found out."[2] In the section borrowed from Shaw Stewart, Nightingale advises the advocates of female nursing to keep their training projects small, expanding them later if they succeed. She expects and anticipates criticism, warning readers that "nothing is more pernicious than to underrate the objections of opponents" (*Subsidiary*, 17). These concerns are also revealed in the text's arguments for anonymity. Publicity can only increase the difficulties of the nursing experiment, Nightingale claims, and her "Introduction to Female Nursing" urges that the profession develop without the burden of public scrutiny: "What is wrong in hospitals is to be patiently, laboriously, and, above all, quietly mended by efforts made within them" (33). With pragmatism and hyperbole, *Subsidiary Notes* observes that "[q]uietness has been from the beginning of its publicity the one thing wanted in this work. I know the fuss, which from its beginning surrounded, was abhorrent to us and was the act of others. But the work, which is all we care for, has throughout suffered from it. It is equally injurious and impeding as regards surgeons, nurses, and people, who are neither. External help in this coarse, repulsive, servile, noble work, for it is all these things, is truly the reed which pierced the hand that leant upon it" (19). The text, far from sanguine, pessimistically counsels readers to keep their expectations for female nursing low: "Let us be prepared, as I know well we must be, for disappointments of every sort and kind. What can any of us do any in anything, what are any of us meant to do in anything, but our duty, leaving the event to God?" (11).

A short, candid footnote to her text reveals part of the reason for Nightingale's pessimism. The note alludes to the problems of her nursing party in Scutari that were "deeply to be regretted": "Rebellion among some ladies and some nuns, and drunkenness among some nurses unhappily disgraced our body; minor faults justified *pro tanto* the common opinion that the vanity, the gossip, and the insubordination . . . of women make them unfit for, and mischievous in the Service" (*Subsidiary*, 28). Although Nightingale had reservations about the usefulness of religious women in hospitals, she observed the benefits of the sisters' chastity and sobriety. Shaw Stewart's section observes that "Sisters of Mercy, as regards the ward service, are decorous and kind, and sometimes inefficient and prudish." Secular nurses are "careful, efficient, often decorous, and always kind, sometimes drunken, sometimes unchaste. Misconduct of women is far more pernicious in a Military or Naval Hospital than in any other, as regards the result of things—the crime is, of course, equally crime everywhere" (17). Such complaints about the behavior of the nurses illustrate the tensions that arose among Nightingale's party in the Crimea. The group of nurses that had been so quickly selected for her came from a cross-section of social and economic backgrounds, and their common uniform could not mask fundamental differences. Misunderstandings arose from anti-Catholic prejudice, and Nightingale complicated the issue when she sought complete authority over the sisters who had pledged obedience to their respective religious orders. After the war, established nursing sisterhoods competed with Nightingale's newly proposed nursing school; the sisterhoods were threatening because they were "the immediate beneficiaries of the public enthusiasm" for military nursing, and they had the support of Dr. Andrew Smith, Nightingale's nemesis at the War Office (*Angels*, 70). Sidney Herbert had promised that all nurses going to the East would be treated equally, thus working-class women felt betrayed when ladies expected them to act as maids and cooks. Well-to-do women were appalled by the "insolent bearing" of lower-class women who worked beside them; in addition, they were mortified by nursing uniforms that made them look like domestics.

As Nightingale supervised this fractious group, she attempted to propagate her conception of nursing as a type of social engineering for women. Religious sisterhoods glorified nursing as an unpaid calling, and they assumed that the class of women who worked for wages lacked the spiritual gifts needed to tend the sick. In contrast, Nightingale envisioned nursing as a profession that, as it became accepted and codified, could provide a living for and improve the status of marginalized women. She notes that "the majority of women in all European countries are, by God's providence, compelled to work for their bread"; the jobs available to them, though, were limited. For the women who "live by their shame," nursing could become an avenue of honest work (*Subsidiary*, 6). Noting that head nurses were currently drawn from "tradesmen's and servants' widows" (34), Nightingale imagines that the women of the tradesman class can be shaped into efficient "Assistant-Nurses." Toward that end, she discusses specific provisions for their salaries, raises, and pensions.

Nurses from the tradesman class would be joined by the daughters of privilege. The text observes that the "real dignity of a gentlewoman is a very high and unassailable thing, which silently encompasses her from her birth to her grave" (*Subsidiary*, 9). Although this regal bearing could bring an important air of credibility to the enterprise, it could also create problems. *Subsidiary Notes* gives a litany of lady nurses' infractions during the Crimean War, summarized by the following: "Obedience, discipline, self-control, work understood as work, hospital service as implying masters, civil and medical, and a mistress, what service means, and abnegation of self, are things not always easy to be learnt, understood, and faithfully acted upon, by ladies" (8). Nightingale's plan for nursing was to incorporate women of the upper class into a training program with their less-privileged sisters. She imagined that ladies' superior education, not their social status, would make them candidates for supervisory positions. In this egalitarian training program, "efficiency would be promoted, sundry things would be checked, and the leaven would circulate." Nightingale acknowledges the prejudice against upper-class women in service, predicting that "the surgeons will dislike these unpaid Nurses . . . the Matron also will not like them, at first," and "the other Nurses will have, at the first, a strong little touch of republicanism towards them" (53). Yet those upper-class women able to adapt to their surroundings, who do "not coldly withdraw from occasional companionship with other Nurses . . . [will] effect quietly a great deal of good" (52).

The middle class, however, offered Nightingale the most hope for the future of nursing. *Subsidiary Notes* predicts that the profession will attract educated women who need to support themselves; most important, middle-class women would provide a buffer between gentlewomen and nurses from the servant class. "These persons would be far more useful, less troublesome, would blend better and more truly with women of the higher orders, who were in the work, and would influence better and more easily the other nurses, as head-nurses, than as ladies" (*Subsidiary*, 8). This prediction was confirmed through experience. The imperious Shaw Stewart, the baronet's daughter, treated her nurses much like servants. She was relieved of her duties as superintendent-general at the military hospital at Netley after a review that questioned the large number of nurses she discharged for violating regulations, such as for exchanging letters with a patient. Her own conduct was questioned, as well: she admitted beating one of her nurses. Her successor, Jane Cecilia Deeble, was an army surgeon's widow whose status threatened neither the medical officers nor her nurses. Whereas the pioneering Shaw Stewart was forced to resign after only six years at the General Hospital at Netley, Deeble served as lady superintendent of the Army Nursing Service from 1870 to 1889.

Although Nightingale pragmatically recognized the "useful" middle class's contributions to nursing, she sided squarely with the concerns of her own class: "[S]he sympathised with the ladies' desire for lower-class women who knew their place" (*Angels*, 59). Her training as a gentle-woman gave her no tolerance for nurses' insubordination; in addition, criticism of those opposing female nursing could be countered only by an emphasis on discipline and order. Nightingale's ambiguous position as wartime superintendent of nurses had brought home to her the need for a clear and unquestioned chain of command. Not until the end of the Crimean War did a military "general order" clarify her authority, confirming that no nurses could be transferred without her approval and that medical officers could direct nurses only through their lady superintendent. *Subsidiary Notes* alludes to her battles with Dr. John Hall, observing, "It is impossible to appoint the work of the Nurses without the concurrence of the Director-General. It does not do to put a woman in a great ward, or several smaller wards, of men, with several orderlies, without clearly defining her position there" (*Subsidiary*, 31).

In creating rules for military hospital wards, Nightingale suggests policies for patients and orderlies that can appear insensitive or extreme. She approves of the civilian hospital plan of saving time by calling patients by numbers rather than by their names, praising the efficiency of London hospitals in which "sometimes a patient's name is never heard in the ward" (*Subsidiary*, 118). She advises a hospital design that eliminates small rooms, warning that such "sculleries" can harbor insurrection. An odd closet can become "a hiding or skulking place for patients or servants disposed to do wrong," she claims, ominously adding that "of such no Hospital will ever be free" (85). She advocates limiting visitors to the venereal wards and praises the "firm and vigilant Head Nurse" who sets aside hospital rules by refusing to admit unsavory visitors such as prostitutes and "procuresses" (117). Some of the impetus for Nightingale's severe approach to ward management derives from details regarding hospital conditions. For example, she advises retaining a policy adopted during the war that prohibits "swearing and indecent language" in hospitals. Her goal is not merely to avoid offending nurses but rather to maintain an appropriate atmosphere in which they can work: "[I]t is not their [nurses'] business to maintain discipline, it is their duty to call in those whose duty it is when discipline is infringed" (119). The condition of the wards she witnessed in Scutari is reflected in her mention of a "coercion apparatus" to treat delirium tremens. Nightingale reveals one of the more challenging duties of the hospital staff when she asserts that "mechanical restraint excites a patient much less, and quiets him much sooner, than the prolonged struggle with his attendant's arms and hands, which *must* otherwise be resorted to" (84).

Subsidiary Notes advocates strict control of the conditions in hospital wards, and suggestions for regulating nurses are equally demanding. Twelve-hour shifts are recommended for night nurses, "with instant dismissal if found asleep" (*Subsidiary*, 12). The need for nurses' sobriety and good character is mentioned repeatedly, and stern punishments are suggested for infractions. "None but women of unblemished character should be suffered to enter the work, and any departure from chastity should be visited with instant final dismissal. . . . The first offence of dishonesty, and,

at the very furthest, the third offence of drunkenness, should ensure irre-
versible dismissal. No nurse dismissed, from whatever cause, should be
suffered to return" (10). In nineteenth-century texts, "alcohol consump-
tion is metonymically connected to an unnameable (sexual) indulgence,"
and Nightingale's repeated warnings against the dire consequences of
unlit corners and undisciplined orderlies "suggest that the unnameable
activities include masturbation and homosexuality as well as heterosexual
liaisons" (*Uneven,* 181). Nightingale is keenly aware of the sexual politics
and pitfalls of bringing women into a military facility, and she emphasizes
strict ward discipline as essential for maintaining her charges' welfare. The
fear of sexual relations between nurses and their patients is so great that
Nightingale advises keeping nurses entirely out of convalescent wards.
Only after female nursing is well established in military hospitals does she
imagine that ambulatory soldiers can be tended by presumably unattrac-
tive, "elderly, still efficient Nurses."[3]

The tone of *Subsidiary Notes* is so embattled that Nightingale even
allows an unflattering realism to creep into her unbounded admiration
for the British soldier. She argues that the soldier is a product of his
environment and must be regulated as much as any other person in a
hospital ward. "The soldier is what, amidst all his faults, he has been
made by the habit and spirit of discipline," she says. "Relax discipline,
and in proportion as you do so, there remains of the soldier a being with
as much or more of the brute than the man" (*Subsidiary,* 37). As it
defends female nursing against its critics, *Subsidiary Notes* asks readers to
put aside political posturing and to remember the soldiers' interests
because "they are worth suffering a good deal for." In this attempt to
soften opposition, the text appeals to a higher authority and asks that
"please God in the long run good will be done. If only we can keep clear
of the false, pernicious, and derogatory system of puffery and fuss . . .
and from vague, silly good-feeling. . . . The purpose is a good and noble
one, and God grant it success!" (53). *Subsidiary Notes* evokes a benison
upon the experiment of female military nursing, and with its depiction
of truculent doctors, defensive War Office administrators, well-meaning
but undisciplined ladies, and sometimes uncooperative working-class
nurses, it indicates the endeavor had need of a blessing.

"You Must Learn to *Manage*": *Notes on Nursing*

Subsidiary Notes is Nightingale's justification and defense of the female
military nurse. In this 1858 government report, the future of female

nursing is uncertain, and her tone is that of one beset by the willful mis-understandings of critics and ill-informed journalists. Soon after pub-lishing this guarded treatise, she brought forth an ebulliently confident and widely regarded text on domestic nursing called *Notes on Nursing: What It Is, and What It Is Not* (1860). This slim volume, aimed at a pop-ular reading audience, sold 15,000 two-shilling copies in only a few months, and her biographer calls it "the best-known, and in some ways, the best, of her books" (*Life*, 1:448). With revisions and additions, the text was repeatedly translated and reissued, its popularity arising, in part, because it was the first book that Nightingale made accessible to the general public. For four years, the public had received little news about the famous nurse, and few people knew of her labor for the gov-ernment since her return from the Crimea. With the publication of this small, readable volume, "here was a book by Florence Nightingale on the very subject to which her fame was attached. The effect produced upon many minds by *Notes on Nursing* was the greater because it came, as it were, as a kind of resurrection of the popular heroine" (*Life*, 1:449).

Notes on Nursing claims not to teach nursing to others but rather to offer "hints for thought to women who have personal charge of the health of others."[4] With this formulaic disclaimer, Nightingale proceeds to speak as an authority on the needs of invalids and the specialized skills required of caretakers. The 40-year-old author refers to her famous wartime exploits when she classifies herself as "an old experienced nurse" who has "herself seen more of what may be called surgical nurs-ing . . . than, perhaps, any one in Europe" (*Nursing*, 156, 210). Nightin-gale adopts the cool voice of the veteran nurse, and in her role as a nurs-ing sage, she extends to the domestic front her battle for improved sanitation. She offers explicit advice on the handling of chamber pots and accompanies her instructions with emphatic margin notes, such as, "Don't make your sick-room into a sewer" (13). Securing what Nightin-gale calls "the health of houses" requires not only vigilant care of cham-ber pots but also keen attention to the quality of air, light, water, and overall hygiene. No detail is too small: Nightingale offers instructions on the proper means of opening windows to prevent drafts, as well as the healthiest type of floor surface.

Although scientists had found increasing evidence that disease was contagious, Nightingale has only contempt for the "infection" theory. She adamantly claims that illness arises spontaneously from unsanitary conditions; indeed, she claims to have smelled smallpox growing. Dark, poorly ventilated rooms are "quite ripe to breed small-pox, scarlet-fever,

diphtheria, or anything else you please" (*Nursing,* 128). Illness is person-
ified as an active, malevolent force that is unleashed by carelessness:
"although we 'nose' the murderers, in the musty unaired unsunned
room, the scarlet fever which is behind the door, or the fever and hospital gangrene which are stalking among the crowded beds of a hospital
ward."

Nightingale was "blindly and fanatically against the germ theory of
infection," and her prejudice appears merely perverse until she arrives at
its logical conclusion: If disease spreads arbitrarily from one person to
another, then what possible purpose could nurses serve?[5] And how could
caregivers be persuaded to put themselves at risk? Nightingale predicts
that if contagion theory were accepted, treatment of patients would
only suffer. She anticipates that doctors, fearful of contracting an illness,
would revert to the medieval practice of examining patients at arm's
length and directing them to lance their own abscesses.

> Does not the popular idea of "infection" involve that people should take
> greater care of themselves than of the patient? that, for instance, it is
> safer not to be too much with the patient, not to attend too much to his
> wants? . . . True nursing ignores infection, except to prevent it. Cleanli-
> ness and fresh air from open windows, with unremitting attention to the
> patient, are the only defence a true nurse either asks or needs.
> Wise and humane management of the patient is the best safeguard
> against infection. (*Nursing,* 142–43)

Belief in contagion theory would grant that disease could spread arbitrarily, a notion that defied all of Nightingale's convictions about sanitation and the need for hospital discipline. To acknowledge contagion
would mean "to deny the possibility of improving hospital conditions
and perhaps even to question the need for the hospital's existence. . . .
Contagion seemed morally random and thus a denial of the traditional
assumption that both health and disease arose from particular states of
moral and social order."[6] For Nightingale, the presence of disease was
nature's indication of a larger problem that could be treated and eliminated by appropriate sanitary principles. Her belief in a divine order led
her to contend that pestilence was God's sign that "certain physical laws"
had been broken (*Nursing,* 136). Sanitation implied control, whereas contagion implied mere chaos. Until the end of her long career, she would
declare that diseases were "adjectives, not noun substantives" (142).

Nightingale's theories on the morality of disease prevention quickly
became dated, even to her contemporaries; in contrast, her observations

regarding patients' mental health anticipate modern theories of psychology. She argues that the mind controls the patient's physical health, and although she can offer only her own experience as proof, her marginal notations insist that "these things are not fancy." "People say the effect [of boredom] is only on the mind. It is no such thing. The effect is on the body, too. Little as we know about the way in which we are affected by form, by colour, and light, we do know this, that they have an actual physical effect" (*Nursing,* 160–61). Patients who are startled or interrupted are subjected to a "new exertion," Nightingale claims, and she offers extensive advice on how to best avoid such annoyances. For example, nurses should carefully avoid surprising patients who are walking about. "A patient in such a state is not going to the East Indies. If you would wait ten seconds, or walk ten yards further, any promenade he could make would be over" (154–55). A chapter titled "Variety" suggests providing patients with music and flowers, bringing infants to visit, or simply positioning the sickbeds near a window. She draws on her own experience of illness during the Crimean War, saying, "I have seen, in fevers, (and felt, when I was a fever patient myself) the most acute suffering produced from a patient (in a hut) not being able to see out of window, and the knots of wood being the only view. I shall never forget the rapture of fever patients over a bunch of bright-coloured flowers. I remember (in my own case) a nosegay of wild flowers being sent me, and from that moment recovery becoming more rapid" (160).

Nightingale's most revealing advice about patients' psychological needs appears in the chapter "Chattering Hopes and Advices," a section that despairs at the conduct of sickbed visitors. She illustrates the frustrating suggestions of ill-informed friends by drawing on her own list of grievances. Although doctors had prescribed bed rest and a strict diet for her condition, her acquaintances thought differently of the matter: "I have been advised to go to every place extant in and out of England— to take every kind of exercise by every kind of cart, carriage—yes, and even swing (!) and dumb-bell (!) in existence; to imbibe every different kind of stimulus that has ever been invented" (*Nursing,* 187). Nightingale finds such unsolicited advice to be, at best, wearisome to the sick; at worst, it is uninformed and impertinent. One of her friends wondered "if the originals will recognize themselves" as portrayed in her text; if so, her cheerful sickbed visitors certainly would have cringed at the review given by their captive audience (*Life,* 1:454): "If . . . the patient says nothing, but the Shakespearian 'Oh!' 'Ah!' 'Go to!' and 'In good sooth!' in order to escape from the conversation about himself the sooner, he is depressed by want of sympathy. He feels isolated in the midst of friends. He feels what a convenience it would be, if there were any single person to whom he could speak simply and openly, without pulling the string upon himself of this shower-bath of silly hopes and encouragements" (*Nursing,* 189).

In her own experience as an invalid, Nightingale sorely felt the want of a champion, a caretaker to protect her from boorish acquaintances and to address her needs "simply and openly." Nightingale's feelings of vulnerability and her annoyance at clumsy care are evident in her text's imperative on "petty management." Because nurses are entrusted with both the physical and emotional charge of their patients, Nightingale argues, they should leave no aspect of the sickroom to chance. Whether nurses are physically present or not, they should take steps to ensure patients receive no unpleasant mail, are not interrupted during sleep, and are not disturbed by strangers. In addition, nurses should avoid annoying the sick by whispering, walking too heavily, or allowing their skirts to rustle: "[A] nurse who rustles . . . is the horror of a patient" (*Nursing,* 152).

Nurses learn to recognize sources of patients' agitation by the skill Nightingale calls "observation." The stated purpose of nurses' observation is to report these findings to the attending physician, but Nightingale's description places much more emphasis on the act of gathering facts than on the transmittal of this information to a doctor.

> [W]ho can have any opinion of any value as to whether the patient is better or worse, excepting the constant medical attendant, or the really observing nurse?
>
> The most important practical lesson that can be given to nurses is to teach them what to observe—how to observe—what symptoms indicate improvement—what the reverse—which are of importance—which are none—which are the evidence of neglect—and of what kind of neglect. (*Nursing,* 194)

Nightingale portrays "observation" not as a passive act but rather as an active, protective vigil. To guard her patients against a potentially fatal chill, "a careful nurse will keep a constant watch over her sick, especially weak, protracted, and collapsed cases"; in delicate cases, patients "should be watched with the greatest care from hour to hour, I had almost said from minute to minute" (131). If necessary, nurses may take notes on, for example, the times that patients can best eat or sleep, or what diversions seem best to cheer or unnecessarily excite them. But if nurses cannot train themselves to notice such details, "you had better give up the being a nurse, for it is not your call, however kind and anxious you may be" (199).

In spite of all her "hints" to her readers, Nightingale indicates that some aspects of observation remain intuitive. In a chapter written for girls on "Minding Baby," she addresses any confusion that may have arisen from her instruction: "Perhaps you will say to me: 'I don't know what you would have me do. You puzzle me so. You tell me don't feed the child too much, and don't feed it too little; don't keep the room shut up, and don't let there be a draught; don't let the child be dull, and don't amuse it too much.' Dear little nurse, you must learn to *manage*. I have felt all these difficulties myself; and I can tell you that it is not from reading my book that you will learn to mind baby well, but from practising yourself how best to manage to do what other good nurses (and in my book if you like it) tell you" (*Nursing,* 219). As they learned the practice of this domestic, womanly observation and "management," nurses would learn to anticipate every need and potential problem; in the process, they would attain complete control of their incapacitated patients. In the name of emotional "management" and elimination of drafts, the nurse brings order not only to a patient's diet and chamber pot but also to visitors, correspondence, and reading material. One critic calls this effect Nightingale's exploitation of the "militaristic component of the domestic ideal," a militancy that also minimized the contributions of medical men (*Uneven,* 188). *Notes on Nursing* emphasizes that nurses are strictly obedient to attending physicians; however, doctors are portrayed as dependent upon the skills of the female "constant medical attendant." The result is an ambiguous illustration of capable, independent nurses that, the author emphasizes, are properly feminine and nonthreatening.

Nightingale struggles to create a space for female nurses within the complicated arena of Victorian sexual politics. Her privileged social status allowed her access to the men who formed public policy. As a product of her social class, she takes pains to distance herself from the "female ink bottles" who agitated for suffrage and equal rights for women, certainly realizing that "she could only have such influence if she did not insist it was due as a matter of political principle" ("Rights," 138). Consequently, she discourages women's entrance into the traditionally male fields of medicine; in a letter to John Stuart Mill, she argues that the pioneering efforts of women doctors, such as Elizabeth Blackwell, have not been successful. "For, mark you, the women have made no improvement—they have only tried to be 'Men,' & they have only succeeded in being third-rate men" (*Ever Yours,* 210). Nightingale gives little encouragement to women doctors, a strategy that encourages women interested in health care to participate instead in her nursing project. To male doctors, she leaves the fields of surgery and medicine, but for women she claims the right to control the sickroom. She launches a "territorial campaign" that ensures nurses' autonomy by insisting on a gendered division of labor for health care (*Uneven* 186).

> It is often said by men, that it is unwise to teach women anything about these laws of health, because they will take to physicking,—that there is a great deal too much of amateur physicking as it is, which is indeed true. . . . There is nothing ever seen in any professional practice like the reckless physicking by amateur females. But this is just what the really experienced and observing nurse does not do; she neither physicks herself nor others. And to cultivate in things pertaining to health observation and experience in women who are mothers, governesses or nurses, is just the way to do away with amateur physicking, and if the doctors did but know it, to make the nurses obedient to them,—helps instead of hindrances. (*Nursing,* 212–13)

In Nightingale's portrayal, nurses are doctors' obedient helpmeets, yet within this sphere, their authority is assured. By foregrounding the gendered parameters of domestic nursing, she effectively removes it from the controversial, highly politicized realm of *Subsidiary Notes.* Emphasis on nurses' character, sobriety, and chastity are no longer necessary because, in the civilian arena, nursing is presented as a "naturally" feminine act: "[E]very woman must, at some time or other of her life, become a nurse, *i.e.,* have charge of somebody's health" (1).

Nightingale avoids overt feminist lobbying for professional equality or suffrage for women, but she advances the equally radical prospect that respectable women can work for wages and manage male patients. She stubbornly insists that nursing must be treated as a profession rather than as simple womanly altruism, rejecting attempts to romanticize the work or to leave it to untrained volunteers.

> It seems a commonly received idea among men and even among women themselves that it requires nothing but a disappointment in love, the want of an object, a general disgust, or incapacity for other things, to turn a woman into a good nurse. This reminds one of the parish where a stupid man was set to be schoolmaster because he was "past keeping the

pigs." . . . Are not these [nursing] matters of sufficient importance and difficulty to require learning by experience and careful inquiry, just as much as any other art? They do not come by inspiration to the lady disappointed in love, nor to the poor workhouse drudge hard up for a livelihood. (*Nursing,* 214–15)

Final pages of *Notes on Nursing* neatly summarize the author's conflicting opinions of women's rights and their place in the health care profession. She first dismisses "jargon," her label for the contemporary discussion that "urges women to do all that men do, including the medical and other professions, merely because men do it, and without regard to whether this *is* the best women can do." Yet she also rejects the notion that women are not suited for some professions, that they can do "nothing that men do, merely because they are women, and should be 'recalled to a sense of their duty as women.' . . . Surely woman should bring the best she has, *whatever* that is, to the work of God's world, without attending to either of these cries" (*Nursing,* 215).

Notes on Nursing covers much more subject matter than its disingenuous title implies. The text is Nightingale's bully pulpit, her most successful attempt to use her popularity to educate the public about sanitation issues and to endorse nursing as an accepted career for educated women. Her brief text on health care is hardly objective; her views on germ theory and on women's role in the sickroom reveal an agenda based on her privileged social class and her political savvy. Her text gave contemporary readers what they wanted: images of attentive bedside ministrations from the heroine of the Crimea. A sympathetic biographer concludes that "it is impossible to doubt, after reading it, that Miss Nightingale was a gentle and sympathetic nurse" (*Florence,* 229). Yet even the Lady with a Lamp responds to social realities, and her careful presentation of the nurse's image— independent yet obedient, assertive yet feminine—show the resulting compromises. In its contradictions and its pragmatism, *Notes on Nursing* reminds readers that Nightingale's battle to improve public health was as much about winning popular opinion as about presenting substantive facts.

Sanitation and "Civilisation": *Observations . . . on the Sanitary State of the Army in India*

Nightingale's writing after her return from the Crimea explores a variety of issues affecting nursing and hospital conditions, but the most ambitious of her projects addresses the condition of the army in India. After 1857, grisly newspaper accounts of violent uprisings by Indian troops and the British army's equally violent reprisals brought the subcontinent to the public's attention. In addition, the rebellion of Indian sepoys required the British army to defend its empire with its own soldiers, and thousands more men were sent abroad. Nightingale's work to improve soldiers' conditions in India illustrates her brilliance as a statistician and administrator, as well as the limitations of her position as an unofficial government advisor. She published numerous pamphlets advocating reform of the Indian taxation system and stressing the importance of irrigation to improve the local diet. Her most impressive publication, though, remained her first, the enormous report issued in 1863 by the Royal Commission on the Sanitary State of the Army in India. She concisely summarized the huge government Blue Book with *Observations on the Evidence Contained in the Stational Reports Submitted to Her by the Royal Commission on the Sanitary State of the Army in India* (1863). From her couch in London, Nightingale made herself an expert on the health and hygiene of Indian military stations and surrounding villages. Her compilation of data provided such a detailed analysis of soldiers' life abroad that "it was said at the time that such a complete picture of life in India, both British and native, was contained in no other book in existence" (*Life*, 1:25).

Following the Sepoy Mutiny, control of India was passed from the East India Company to the British Crown. As the government took responsibility for thousands more soldiers abroad, accounts of conditions at military bases raised concerns about the health of troops stationed there. Avoidable disease caused by poor sanitation practices cost the army an estimated £388,000 per year; before improvements were made, Nightingale claimed that the mortality rate of the army in India was as high as 69 deaths per 1,000.[7] Soldiers' wives and children also suffered from poor sanitation, and Nightingale compared their losses from disease to the lives lost during the uprising. Because of the overcrowded conditions at the military station of Dumdum, the mortality rate of the 554 women and 770 children living there was six times that of soldiers' families in Bengal: "[W]hile the husbands were punishing the murderers of English women and children in the upper provinces, their own wives and children were being destroyed in vast numbers, for want of care. . . . If one-tenth of the calamity had happened in England, there would have been coroners' inquests over and over again, and public opinion, if not law, would have punished some one. At Dumdum the enquiry took place after the destruction of human life had been going on for months."[8] Nightingale agitated for a royal commission to investigate sanitation in India, and in 1859 she convinced her friend Lord Stanley, the secretary of the Indian Office, to form one. With the assistance of such well-placed acquaintances, Nightingale's participation was much as it had been in 1857, when she had prodded the government committee to investigate hospitals in the Crimea. She anticipated that the projects would be similar, writing to Harriet Martineau that the newly formed commission would "do exactly the same thing for the Armies in India which the last did for the Army at home" (*Ever Yours,* 204).

The most obvious contrast between Nightingale's work on the two royal commissions was the difference in the experience she brought to her work. Her opinions about military hospitals were based on her 18 months in the Crimea, but she had never set foot in India. Her attempt to educate herself about the army's condition was made more difficult by the lack of accurate data on the military stations. Nightingale needed specific, detailed information regarding military outposts, information that could be obtained only from observers in the field. She set about getting these details by drawing up a painstakingly detailed, nine-page questionnaire that asserted: "Answers are required by the Commissioners from every Station throughout India and its Dependencies." Her "circular of inquiry" contained 175 questions that covered topography, climate, and sanitary conditions. It asked for each military station to return its regulations for sanitary practices, sketches of its barracks and hospitals, and an extensive meteorological table "for as many years past as possible." She asked about the condition and location of cesspits; she wanted to know how each station's drinking water tasted and smelled; she inquired where the station's dead were buried and the depth of their graves. The returns also asked officers to compare their experiences at different stations. Nightingale was thus satisfied that "in this manner there has been collected together the Indian experience of nearly every regiment there at the time, on every point bearing on the soldiers' health, whether relating to climate, locality, barracks and hospitals, diet, habits, or duties."[9] Nightingale always regretted that she never traveled to India, but the stational returns provided her with a lasting image of the country. Years later, she recalled the "mass of documentary evidence which few in India and very few in England have seen. India has been familiar to me for more than twenty years from documents—the plain unvarnished evidence of plain witnesses."[10] During the years before she went "out of office," it was the custom for Indian officials to visit Miss

Nightingale before their departure to be tutored on the contents of her commission report and to hear her suggestions for reform.

An enormous amount of work was required by the witnesses who completed Nightingale's demanding "circular of inquiry," yet of the 175 stations that received the questionnaire, two-thirds returned it with the desired information. The result was a mountain of paper that filled an entire room in Nightingale's house and took her three years to analyze. Together with the sanitarian Dr. John Sutherland and the statistician Dr. William Farr, Nightingale compiled the two-volume, 2,028-page Blue Book that presented the findings of her "circular"; the second volume was composed entirely of the collected data. Nightingale's *Observations* was included in the original report, and Farr was particularly pleased with her effort, writing to Sutherland, "Miss Nightingale's Paper is a masterpiece, in her best style; and will rile the enemy very considerable—all for his good, poor creature" (*Life*, 1:26). One provoked "enemy" may have retaliated, because Nightingale's summary of the commission's findings was inexplicably omitted from the abbreviated commission report circulated in Parliament. In response, Sutherland and Farr had Nightingale's text published separately with woodcut illustrations. An intense media campaign ensured that both volumes were heavily puffed in the popular press by journalists such as Martineau, and Nightingale's biographer observes that "[n]one of Miss Nightingale's official works obtained a wider circulation than the *Observations*; nor, I suppose, did any Blue-book on such a subject ever attain a greater amount of publicity" (2:38).

Nightingale's *Observations* was sure to "rile" the sanitarians' opposition with its disquieting evidence regarding soldiers' living conditions. Sanitary defects in India were much like the ones she had witnessed in the Crimea: Camp diseases arose from poor water, drainage, and ventilation, as well as overcrowding and unsanitary conditions in surrounding villages. The text is startling, though, in its illustrations from the station reports, the voices of the military camps that spoke from Nightingale's mountain of paper: "Chunar says that its water is clear, sweet, and inodorous 'if allowed to settle before it is drunk.' Agra's water is 'laxative,' and 'apt to disagree *at first*.' Dinapore admits that its wells have been poisoned by infiltration from barrack privies. Nusserabad says, 'The flavour (of the water) varies according to the quantity of the salts.' At Murree the quality is 'considered inferior by native visitors, and to cause colic' "(*Observations*, 4). Camps' drainage systems are submitted to the same scrutiny as their water sources. The distasteful secrets of the army's cesspools are discussed at length, illustrated by layouts of barrack lavatories and elevations of latrines. The reporter at a station at Hyderabad finds the camp's sanitary state "in every respect, satisfactory," but Nightingale reveals how the reporter's own evidence contradicts his assessment: "The contents of the cesspits are 'thrown about in close vicinity to the cesspits.' 'Anything edible is immediately picked up by birds or dogs.' There is 'great room for reform' in the native latrines, the cleansing of which consists mainly in the liquid 'sinking into the subsoil, so that the earth is thoroughly saturated, and a *noisome odour pervades* the atmosphere'" (12). *Observations* grimly cites reports of human refuse thrown "over the fort wall," carried away in tubs, or simply spread over the ground to dry. Nightingale asserts that she has not tried to horrify her readers by selecting the stations' most egregious examples of sanitary abuse. She closes a section on "Bad Drainage" by finding that "[i]t is impossible to pursue this subject further. There are such much worse things in the Stational Reports than what I have chosen to give, that I must say to those who call my 'bonnet ugly,' 'There are much uglier bonnets to be had'" (18). She repeatedly refers skeptical readers to the 2,028-page report for "further and fouler evidence" (22).

Nightingale incorporated her system of morality into her guidelines for nursing, and she similarly stresses that morals must be considered in improving the sanitation of barracks. A section of her query to military stations is devoted to "Intemperance"; here, she inquires about the availability of spirits in the camp and neighboring villages. *Observations* criticizes the army's canteen system, which provides liquor for soldiers on the theory that it will be safer than liquor from local bazaars. The text satirically notes that "if the facilities for washing were as great as those for drink, our Indian army would be the cleanest body of men in the world" (*Observations*, 10). Her records reveal the number of soldiers arrested for "habitual drunkenness" and the number admitted to hospitals for delirium tremens; she reports an "average of habitual drunkards in some European regiments not less than 15 per cent" (32–33). Nightingale suggests providing soldiers with less potent spirits, such as malt liquor instead of gin or rum; less realistically, she predicts that "it will be a 'happy day' when nothing but beer, light wines, coffee, tea, lemonade, [etc.] are to be sold" in army canteens (34).

Soldiers' drinking is blamed in part on their lack of recreation; Nightingale is appalled by their inactivity. She asserts that men would benefit from increased discipline, finding that "so unaccustomed is the soldier to ordinary exertion that, as might be expected, the short

parades are talked of as injurious, as if they were long harassing
marches, while, curiously enough, it is admitted that the soldier is never
better than when he is exposed to the harass and fatigue of field service"
(*Observations*, 44). She illustrates the idle soldiers with a woodcut of men
smoking and playing cards in their barracks, apparently at much risk to
their health. Nightingale's inexperience with the Indian climate is
revealed in complaints that soldiers remain in their barracks to escape
the heat. She is aghast that "Cawnpore actually orders the men to be
confined to barracks for 10 hours a day in hot weather. . . . Yet Chunar's
mean temperature is 65° in December and 92° in June, its sun temperature as high as 120° in June. And yet the men do not 'suffer from exposure' " (45).

A lazy, intemperate army cannot be a healthy one, Nightingale
argues. A later text asserts that introducing female nurses to India will
improve the country's moral fiber, claiming that "no one, probably, who
is acquainted with European life in India will doubt that such a continu-
ous stream of fresh blood and advanced knowledge will be necessary to
prevent progressive deterioration."[11] The contrast between European
advancement and India's "defective civilisation" is seen in Nightingale's
condemnation of the "antique system" of hiring Indian villagers to transport water. She even includes woodcuts of "bheesties" to ensure that
readers appreciate the difficulty of carrying water in a leather skin on
one's back. Such a practice, Nightingale argues, would invite water carri-
ers to collect water from the nearest source rather than the most pure
one; she suggests that "water-pipes without a will" would be safer (*Observations*, 6–7). The condemnation of "water-pipes" is one of Nightingale's
many appeals to her readers' Eurocentrism, and she complains of the
complacency with which reporters describe "water sources, qualities, and
modes of distribution which civilised cities have ceased to use" (8).

In Nightingale's analysis, the sanitary condition of local villages is
not the result of poverty or economic exploitation but rather of imper-
fect imperialism. Her report on conditions of local villages exclaims,
"can it be possible that such a state of things exists after all these years
of possession and unlimited authority?" (*Observations*, 76). *Observations*
equates sanitation with "civilisation," implying that health is a European construct independent of social, economic, or geographical concerns. As a result, local practices are seen only as backward or illogical,
such as the traditional custom of varnishing earth floors with cow dung.
Nightingale's report resorts to sarcasm, observing that "like Mahomet
and the mountain, if men won't go to the dunghill, the dunghill, it

appears, comes to them." Her dismissal of the practice, however, appeals to readers' logic: "[I]t is not economical for Government to make the soldiers as uncivilised as possible. Nature sends in her bill—a bill which always has to be paid—and at a pretty high rate of interest too" (31).

Nightingale's writings on nursing and Indian sanitation are an ambiguous combination of her upper-class bias, her farsighted belief in the importance of public health, and her complicated, often contradictory attempts to maneuver her highly political projects past resistant government administrators. Using the models of logic, sacrifice, and control, Nightingale attempted to appropriate male authority for a female field; the results of her pioneering effort, however, could only be limited. Class differences, sexism, and her own independence assured that Nightingale could not cooperate with other nursing leaders to "enlarge or consolidate their power." As a result, one critic observes, nursing remained a secondary occupation that "demonstrated the limitations of a separate female world that lacked an effective power base within its own domain" (*Independent,* 120). Similarly, the results of her unofficial position in directing Indian sanitation reforms would be controlled by budget concerns and administrative infighting. Nightingale was "governess of the governors of India," but her enormous, masterfully wrought collection of evidence could not be transmitted easily into action. She reminded herself that "reports are not self-executive," and although government officials agreed with the recommendations, they seldom acted on them. One critic observes that "[m]ost of the British in India seem so aware of the difficulties of enforcing any legal changes that involved a change in religious practice, that they simply preferred a policy of hands-off, no matter how high the death rates were."[12]

Nightingale often lamented the disparity between her ambitious plans—a complete reform of sanitation in India or a widespread system of trained nurses in military hospitals—and the seemingly minor changes that arose from her detailed research and time-consuming administrative finesse. During her work with the India Office, she shares her disappointments with her confidante Benjamin Jowett. In a painful letter of 1865, Nightingale confesses that "I mar the work of God by my impatience & discontent. . . . I lost my serenity some years ago— then I lost clearness of perception, so that sometimes I did not know whether I was doing right or wrong for two minutes together." Yet Nightingale's admission is followed by her justification, one that rationalizes both the unusual turns of her life and the ambitious scope of her projects:

Only I would say that my life having been a fever, not even a fitful one, is not my own fault. Neck or nothing has been all my public life. It has never been in my power to arrange my work. No more than I could help having to receive & provide for 4000 patients in 17 days (in the Crimean War, and how easy that was compared with what has happened since!) Could I help—in the two R. [Royal] Commissions I have served, in the 9 years I have served the W.O. [War Office]—exclusive of the Crimean War—my whole life being a hurry: if the thing were not done to the day it would not be done at all. . . . Patients won't wait to die, or better, to be made to live. (*Jowett's Letters,* 62)

Though she lived in a "fever," social realities and her own human failings ensured that Nightingale's aspirations would always exceed her tangible accomplishments. Yet even the critical observer F. B. Smith finds that "in India tens of thousands continued to die each year from malnutrition, typhoid fever and cholera, but thousands more lived because Miss Nightingale coached successive Secretaries of State, Viceroys and local medical men in what had to be done and how it could be done" (*Reputation,* 148). Perhaps her greatest achievement, after all, was one of imagination. In enormous texts such as her royal commission reports or her suggestions for domestic nurses, Nightingale examines suffering of individuals in different circumstances, and she offers a vision of healing and change. Sensationalist Victorian journalism and overwrought hagiography helped win Nightingale her reputation as the saintly Lady with a Lamp; the scope of her ambitious failure should win her our respect.

Notes and References

Chapter One

1. Edward Cook, *The Life of Florence Nightingale* (1913; reprint, New York: Macmillan, 1942), 1:234. Hereafter cited in text as *Life*.

2. Nancy Boyd, *Three Victorian Women Who Changed Their World: Josephine Butler, Octavia Hill, Florence Nightingale* (Oxford: Oxford Univ. Press, 1982), 187. Hereafter cited in text as *Victorian Women*.

3. For further discussion of the nineteenth century's transition from domestic nursing to institutionalized, hospital nursing, see Anne Summers, "The Mysterious Demise of Sarah Gamp: The Domiciliary Nurse and Her Detractors, c. 1830–1860," *Victorian Studies* 32 (1989). Hereafter cited in text as "Gamp."

4. "Ballad to Florence Nightingale," cited in Janet H. Murray, *Strong Minded Women, and Other Lost Voices from Nineteenth-Century England* (New York: Pantheon, 1982), 301.

5. Monica Baly, ed., *As Miss Nightingale Said . . . Florence Nightingale through Her Sayings—a Victorian Perspective* (London: Scutari Press, 1991), 104. Hereafter cited in text as *Miss Nightingale Said*.

6. Vincent Quinn and John Prest, eds., *Dear Miss Nightingale: A Selection of Benjamin Jowett's Letters to Florence Nightingale, 1860–1893* (Oxford: Clarenden Univ. Press, 1987), 75, 224. Hereafter cited in text as *Jowett's Letters*.

7. Sue M. Goldie, ed., *"I Have Done My Duty": Florence Nightingale in the Crimean War, 1854–1856* (Iowa City: Univ. of Iowa Press, 1987), 222. Hereafter cited in text as *Duty*.

8. Lois Maunder, ed., *Letters of Florence Nightingale in the History of Nursing Archive, Special Collections, Boston University Libraries* (Boston: Boston Univ. Press, 1974), 51.

9. Mary Poovey, ed., *"Cassandra" and Other Selections from "Suggestions for Thought"* (New York: New York Univ. Press, 1992), 205. Hereafter cited in text as *Cassandra*.

10. "Florence Nightingale as a Leader in the Religious and Civic Thought of Her Time," *Hospitals: The Journal of the American Hospital* 10 (1936): 81.

11. Martha Vicinus and Bea Nergaard, eds., *Ever Yours, Florence Nightingale: Selected Letters* (Cambridge: Harvard Univ. Press, 1990). Hereafter cited in text as *Ever Yours*.

12. Two editions of travel letters are Mary Keele, ed., *Florence Nightingale in Rome: Letters Written by Florence Nightingale in Rome in the Winter of 1847–1848* (Philadelphia: American Philosophical Society, 1981), hereafter

cited in text as *Nightingale in Rome;* and Antony Sattin, ed., *Letters from Egypt: A Journey on the Nile, 1849–1850* (London: Barrie & Jenkins, 1987), hereafter cited in text as *Egypt.* Nightingale's war correspondence is collected in Goldie's *"I Have Done My Duty."*

13.   Michael Calabria and Janet Macrae, eds., *"Suggestions for Thought" by Florence Nightingale: Selections and Commentaries* (Philadelphia: Univ. of Pennsylvania Press, 1994), hereafter cited in text as *Suggestions.* This edition contains a useful introduction to the Victorian religious debate. Mary Poovey's *"Cassandra" and Other Selections from "Suggestions for Thought"* contains the complete text of "Cassandra."

14.   See *The History of Nursing: An Index to the Microfiche Collection,* vol. 1, *The Adelaide Nutting Historical Nursing Collection* (Ann Arbor: University Microfilms International, 1983). The collection includes the complete three-volume text of *Suggestions for Thought,* as well as early Nightingale biographies and related texts.

Chapter Two

1.   Cecil Woodham-Smith, *Florence Nightingale, 1820–1910* (1951; reprint, New York: Atheneum, 1983), 12. Hereafter cited in text as *Florence.*

2.   Anne Summers argues that the wholesale defamation of Victorian nurses' characters stems in part from the threat that such independent nurses presented to physicians' livelihood. See "The Mysterious Demise of Sarah Gamp," 365–86.

3.   Ida B. O'Malley, *Florence Nightingale, 1820–1856: A Study of Her Life Down to the End of the Crimean War* (London: Butterworth, 1931), 125. Hereafter cited in text as *Study.*

4.   James Buzard, *The Beaten Track: European Tourism, Literature, and the Ways to Culture, 1800–1918* (Oxford: Oxford Univ. Press, Clarendon, 1993), 133.

5.   Charlotte A. Eaton, *Rome in the Nineteenth Century,* 5th ed., 2 vols. (London: Henry G. Bohn, 1852), 1:426.

6.   William Makepeace Thackeray, *The Newcomes: Memoirs of a Most Respectable Family* (1856; reprint, London: Smith, Elder, 1884), 1:465.

7.   For more on Victorian sisterhoods, see Martha Vicinus, "Church Communities: Sisterhoods and Deaconesses' Houses," in *Independent Women: Work and Community for Single Women, 1850–1920* (Chicago: Univ. of Chicago Press, 1985). Hereafter cited in text as *Independent.*

8.   Quoted in Cook, *The Life of Florence Nightingale,* 1:75. In *The Making of Italy, 1815–1870* (New York: Atheneum, 1971), Edgar Holt argues that the public "read more into [the pope's] modest and well-meaning gestures than they were meant to convey" (121).

9.   James Pope-Hennessy, *Monckton Milnes: The Years of Promise, 1809–1851* (London: Constable, 1949), 307.

10. John Barrell, "Death on the Nile: Fantasy and the Literature of Tourism, 1840–1860," *Essays in Criticism* 41 (1991): 97. Hereafter cited in text as "Death."

11. *Punch* 14 (1848): 169. Quoted in Buzard, *The Beaten Track,* 322–23.

12. I. Gardner Wilkinson, *Handbook for Travellers in Egypt* (London: John Murray, 1858), xxiii.

13. Nightingale's Egyptian diaries are housed in the British Library. Excerpts are divided among the Cook, Woodham-Smith, and O'Malley biographies, as well as the Vicinus and Nergaard selection of letters.

14. For summaries of Nightingale's letters from Greece, see Sue Goldie and W. J. Bishop, eds., *A Calendar of the Letters of Florence Nightingale* (Oxford: Oxford Microform Publications for the Wellcome Institute for the History of Medicine, 1983).

Chapter Three

1. Poovey, *Cassandra,* 109. Poovey's edition of Nightingale's text focuses on feminist arguments and includes the entire text of "Cassandra." I have cited the Poovey edition when possible. The entire text of *Suggestions for Thought to the Searchers after Truth among the Artizans of England* (London: Eyre & Spottiswoode, 1860) is available on microfiche in the Adelaide Nutting Historical Nursing Collection.

2. Elaine Showalter, "Florence Nightingale's Feminist Complaint: Women, Religion, and *Suggestions for Thought,*" *Signs* 6 (1981): 397.

3. Florence Nightingale, *Suggestions for Thought,* 2:iii. This citation is from the microfiche copy, which comes from the manuscript owned by Nightingale's great-niece Rosalind Vaughn Nash.

4. W. J. Bishop and Sue Goldie, comps. *A Bio-Bibliography of Florence Nightingale* (London: Dawsons of Pall Mall, 1962), 122. Hereafter cited in text as *Bio-Bibliography.* See Florence Nightingale, "A 'Note' of Interrogation," *Fraser's Magazine,* n.s., 7 (1873): 567–77, hereafter cited in text as "Interrogation"; and Nightingale, "A Sub-note of Interrogation: What Will Our Religion Be in 1999?" *Fraser's Magazine,* n.s., 8 (1873): 25–36.

5. Quinn and Prest note that Nightingale sent copies of her manuscript to her father; her uncle Sam Smith; her former fiance, Richard Monckton Milnes; the physician Sir John McNeill; and Benjamin Jowett, who later became master of Balliol College (*Dear Miss Nightingale,* xii). In addition, Showalter ("Florence Nightingale's Feminist Complaint," 407) notes that J. A. Froude, historian and editor of *Fraser's Magazine,* was one of Nightingale's readers.

6. Quoted in Evelyn L. Pugh, "Florence Nightingale and J. S. Mill Debate Women's Rights," *Journal of British Studies* 21 (1982): 128. Hereafter cited in text as "Rights."

7. Cook, *The Life of Florence Nightingale,* 1:471. See also Pugh, "Florence Nightingale and J. S. Mill Debate Women's Rights."

8. Janet Larson, "Lady Wrestling for the Victorian Soul: Discourse, Gender, and Spirituality in Women's Texts," *Religion and Literature* 23 (1991): 56. Hereafter cited in text as "Lady Wrestling."

9. Quoted in Katherine Snyder, "From Novel to Essay: Gender and Revision in Florence Nightingale's 'Cassandra,' " in *The Politics of the Essay: Feminist Perspectives*, ed. Ruth-Ellen Boetcher Joeres and Elizabeth Mittman (Bloomington: Indiana Univ. Press, 1993), 27. Hereafter cited in text as "Novel."

10. See Snyder's discussion of Nightingale's revision of a female genre. She observes that Nightingale's male reviewers were disquieted by the essay format and suggested that she return to the novel form. "Without the mediation of the novel's characters, the essay's unveiled account of women's confinement . . . seemed to her contemporary male readers like indecent exposure" (Snyder, "Novel," 25).

11. Christine Krueger, *The Reader's Repentance: Women Preachers, Women Writers, and Nineteenth-Century Social Discourse* (Chicago: Univ. of Chicago Press, 1992), 9.

12. George P. Landow, "Aggressive (Re)interpretations of the Female Sage: Florence Nightingale's 'Cassandra,' " in *Victorian Sages and Cultural Discourse: Renegotiating Gender and Power*, ed. Thaïs Morgan (New Brunswick: Rutgers Univ. Press, 1990), 41. Hereafter cited in text as "Sage."

13. Cited in JoAnn G. Widerquist, " 'Dearest Rev'd Mother,' " in *Florence Nightingale and Her Era: A Collection of New Scholarship*, ed. Vern Bullough, Bonnie Bullough, and Marietta P. Stanton (New York: Garland, 1990), 302.

14. Quoted in JoAnn G. Widerquist, "The Spirituality of Florence Nightingale," *Nursing Research* 41 (1992): 49, hereafter cited in text as "Spirituality." Here, the phrase "man must create mankind" comes from a letter Nightingale wrote to her father in September 1863.

Chapter Four

1. Florence Nightingale, *Florence Nightingale at Harley Street,* intro. Sir Harry Verney (London: Dent, 1970), 18. Hereafter cited in text as *Harley Street.*

2. John Sweetman, *War and Administration: The Significance of the Crimean War for the British Army* (Edinburgh: Scottish Academic Press, 1984), 47.

3. Christopher Hibbert, *The Destruction of Lord Raglan: A Tragedy of the Crimean War, 1854–1855* (London: Longman's, 1961), 160. Hereafter cited in text as *Raglan.*

4. "Arrival of the Wounded in the Bosphorus," *Times* (London), 9 October 1854, p. 8, col. b; *Times* (London) 12 October 1854.

5. *Hansard's Parliamentary Debates*, 3d ser., 136 (London: Cornelius Buck, 1855), 1136. Hereafter cited in text as *Hansard's.*

6. Quoted in Florence Nightingale, *Notes on Matters Affecting the Health, Efficiency, and Hospital Administration of the British Army, Founded Chiefly*

on the Experience of the Late War (London: Harrison, 1858), 92, hereafter cited in text as *Notes*. The microfilm copy consulted for this study is from the Adelaide Nutting Historical Nursing Collection. This copy was presented to Sir Robert Rawlinson, an engineer who served on the Sanitary Commission sent to the Crimea by Parliament.

7. F. B. Smith, *Florence Nightingale: Reputation and Power* (New York: St. Martin's, 1982), 27. Hereafter cited in text as *Reputation*.

8. "Ballad to Florence Nightingale," cited in Murray, *Strong Minded Women*, 301.

9. Anthony Sterling, *The Story of the Highland Brigade in the Crimea* (London: Macqueen, 1895), 208.

10. Joseph O. Baylen and Alan Conway, eds. *Soldier-Surgeon: The Crimean War Letters of Dr. Douglas A. Reid, 1855–1856* (Knoxville: Univ. of Tennessee Press, 1968), 20.

11. Mary Ann Coyle, 5 December [1854]; quoted in Smith, *Reputation and Power*, 39.

12. Goldie notes the conflicts Nightingale created with doctors through her "remarkable lack of tact" (*Duty*, 128).

13. Nursing historian Anne Summers observes Nightingale's unfair criticism of other nurses who served in the Crimea, finding that she "libelled the ladies and sisters at every opportunity; the power of her pen is such that the accusations of incompetence, spiritual interference, filth and neurosis are still current in the literature," *Angels and Citizens: British Women as Military Nurses, 1854–1914* (London: Routledge & Kegan Paul, 1988), 52, hereafter cited in text as *Angels*. Smith's iconoclastic account in *Reputation and Power* portrays Nightingale as a manipulative, ambitious political animal.

14. Bishop and Goldie, *Bio-Bibliography*, 53.

15. *Notes*, 3:x. Nightingale quotes extensively from appendix 79 of the royal commission report on army sanitation, military correspondence that became available only after *Notes* was in proof sheets. She explains that "I have prefixed to several Sections a classified abstract of the principal documents, not only as confirmatory of the statements I have made in the text but as indicating the administrative changes necessary for preventing similar calamities" (preface). The addition of this material resulted in what Bishop and Goldie call the text's "erratic pagination," in which the correspondence is numbered by Roman numerals (*Bio-Bibliography*, 53). When citations are made from this correspondence, I have indicated the section to which the correspondence is appended.

16. Mary Poovey, *Uneven Developments* (Chicago: Univ. of Chicago Press, 1988), 187. Hereafter cited in text as *Uneven*.

17. See for example the report of Reid, an assistant surgeon: "I have been obliged to get rid of my batman (groom that means) for stealing a pair of boots. My other servant jobs on pretty well but is inclined to get boozy occa-

sionally. . . . By the bye, we shall have a grand dinner, 22 of us sit down and the dinner will cost about £100" (*Notes*, 126).

Chapter Five

1. George Pickering, *The Creative Malady* (New York: Oxford Univ. Press, 1974), 167.

2. Florence Nightingale, *Subsidiary Notes as to the Introduction of Female Nursing into Military Hospitals in Peace and in War*, in *Selected Writings of Florence Nightingale*, ed. Lucy Ridgely Seymer (New York: Macmillan, 1954), 5, hereafter cited in text as *Subsidiary*. Although texts in Seymer's edition often are abridged, this version of Nightingale's work is cited when possible because it is more widely available to readers.

3. *Subsidiary Notes as to the Introduction of Female Nursing into Military Hospitals in Peace and in War* (London: Harrison, 1858), 95. This citation is from the microfiche of Robert Rawlinson's copy of *Subsidiary Notes*, which is included in the Adelaide Nutting Historical Nursing Collection.

4. Florence Nightingale, *Notes on Nursing: What It Is, and What It Is Not* (London: Harrison, 1859; reprint, Philadelphia: Stern, 1946), 1. This citation is from Nightingale's preface, which is not included in the Seymer collection of Nightingale's writing. The Seymer text contains the additional chapter, "Minding Baby," which was included in later editions. When possible, the more widely available Seymer edition is cited in text (as *Nursing*).

5. Monica E. Baly, *Florence Nightingale and the Nursing Legacy* (London: Croom Helm, 1986), 23.

6. Charles E. Rosenberg, "Florence Nightingale on Contagion: The Hospital as Moral Universe," in *Healing and History*, ed. Charles E. Rosenberg (New York: Dawson, 1979), 117.

7. Smith emphasizes that estimates for the army's mortality varied widely. Doctors in India defended their professional reputation by providing figures as low as 20 deaths per 1,000. Smith notes that Nightingale's statistics omitted the Madras and Bengal presidencies because figures were not available, and he argues that her mortality rates are thus inflated. See Smith, *Reputation and Power*, 122–23.

8. Florence Nightingale, *Observations on the Evidence Contained in the Stational Reports Submitted to Her by the Royal Commission on the Sanitary State of the Army in India* (London: Stanford, 1863), 84–85. This microfiche copy of the text is from the Adelaide Nutting Historical Nursing Collection. Hereafter cited in text as *Observations*.

9. *Royal Commission on the Sanitary State of the Army in India. Report of the Commissioners. Précis of Evidence. Minutes of Evidence. Addenda.* (London: Spottis-woode, 1863) 2:1, 1:371. This microfiche copy of the commission report is from the Adelaide Nutting Historical Nursing Collection.

10. Florence Nightingale, "The Dumb Shall Speak and the Deaf Shall Hear: Or the Ryot, the Zemidar and the Government," *Journal of the East India Association* 15 (1883): 169.

11. Florence Nightingale, *Suggestions on a System of Nursing for Hospitals in India* (1865). This citation is from the Seymer edition, 230.

12. Martha Vicinus, private correspondence, quoted in Poovey, *Cassandra*, 245.

Selected Bibliography

PRIMARY SOURCES

Published Works

As Miss Nightingale Said . . . Florence Nightingale through Her Sayings—a Victorian Perspective, ed. Monica Baly. London: Scutari Press, 1991. Baly's edition contains excerpts from Nightingale's publications and private notes, arranged by subject matter.

"Cassandra" and Other Selections from "Suggestions for Thought," ed. Mary Poovey. NYU Press Women's Classics. New York: New York Univ. Press, 1992. Poovey's edition of *Suggestions* contains many of Nightingale's more feminist arguments from the second book of *Suggestions*; in addition, it contains the complete version of the essay "Cassandra."

The History of Nursing: An Index to the Microfiche Collection. Vol. 1, *The Adelaide Nutting Historical Nursing Collection.* Ann Arbor: University Microfilms International, 1983. This index provides a listing of Nightingale's work available on microfiche. The Nutting Collection includes the complete texts of many of her works, including *Suggestions for Thought*; *Notes on Matters Affecting the Health, Efficiency, and Hospital Administration of the British Army*; and *Observations on the Evidence Contained in the Stational Reports Submitted to Her by the Royal Commission on the Sanitary State of the Army in India.* The collection also contains secondary materials, such as early Nightingale biographies and government reports on the Crimean War.

Selected Writings of Florence Nightingale, ed. Lucy Ridgely Seymer. New York: Macmillan, 1954. Seymer's edition provides excerpts from nine Nightingale selections, including *Notes on Nursing* and *Subsidiary Notes as to the Introduction of Female Nursing into Military Hospitals in Peace and in War.*

"Suggestions for Thought" by Florence Nightingale: Selections and Commentaries, ed. Michael D. Calabria and Janet A. Macrae. Univ. of Pennsylvania Press Studies in Health, Illness and Caregiving. Philadelphia: Univ. of Pennsylvania Press, 1994. Calabria and Macrae's edition of *Suggestions* focuses on Nightingale's theology, contextualizing her writing within the Victorian debate over religion.

Letters

A Calendar of the Letters of Florence Nightingale, ed. Sue Goldie and W. J. Bishop. Oxford: Oxford Microform Publications for the Wellcome Institute for

the History of Medicine, 1983. This microfiche guide to Nightingale's
enormous body of letters arranges them chronologically and provides
summaries of their contents. The printed 41-page introduction to the
microfilm includes a listing of libraries with collections of Nightingale
letters, as well as a genealogy of the Smith, Shore, and Verney families.

Dear Miss Nightingale: A Selection of Benjamin Jowett's Letters to Florence Nightingale, 1860–1893, ed. Vincent Quinn and John Prest. Oxford: Clarendon
Univ. Press, 1987. Most of the letters in this edition are Jowett's, and his
correspondence contains both thoughtful theological discussion and inti-
mate, irreverent banter.

Ever Yours, Florence Nightingale: Selected Letters, ed. Martha Vicinus and Bea Nergaard. Cambridge: Harvard Univ. Press, 1990. Vicinus and Nergaard's
edition is the most comprehensive collection of Nightingale letters. The
commentary and the annotations to the letters make this edition both
accessible and fascinating.

*Florence Nightingale in Rome: Letters Written by Florence Nightingale in Rome in the
Winter of 1847–1848,* ed. Mary Keele. Philadelphia: American Philosophical Society, 1981. Keele's edition contains letters from Nightingale's trip
to Rome and a useful introduction into the politics of the Papal States.

"I Have Done My Duty": Florence Nightingale in the Crimean War, 1854–1856, ed.
Sue Goldie. Iowa City, Univ. of Iowa Press, 1987. Goldie's edition provides commentary and contexualization of Nightingale's letters to her
family, Sidney Herbert, and other War Office officials.

Letters from Egypt: A Journey on the Nile, 1849–1850, ed. Antony Sattin. London:
Barrie & Jenkins, 1987. Nightingale's letters are illustrated by paintings
by nineteenth-century artists.

SECONDARY SOURCES

Books and Parts of Books

Baly, Monica E. *Florence Nightingale and the Nursing Legacy.* London: Croom
Helm, 1986. Baly traces the founding and development of the Nightingale Nursing School.

Bishop, W. J., and Sue Goldie, comps. *A Bio-Bibliography of Florence Nightingale.*
London: Dawsons of Pall Mall, 1962. Bishop and Goldie offer an indispensable guide to Nightingale's writing that provides the publishing history of texts and a description of various editions, as well as excerpts and
critical summaries of her writings.

Boyd, Nancy. *Three Victorian Women Who Changed Their World: Josephine Butler,
Octavia Hill, Florence Nightingale.* Oxford: Oxford Univ. Press, 1982.
Boyd's biography offers an excellent discussion of Nightingale's spiritual
life and of *Suggestions for Thought.*

Cook, Edward. *The Life of Florence Nightingale*. 1913. Reprint, New York: Macmillan, 1942. Cook's account is the standard Nightingale biography; it is comprehensive but also subjective.

Landow, George P. "Aggressive (Re)interpretations of the Female Sage: Florence Nightingale's 'Cassandra.' " In *Victorian Sages and Cultural Discourse: Renegotiating Gender and Power*, ed. Thaïs Morgan. New Brunswick: Rutgers Univ. Press, 1990. Landow reads "Cassandra" in the tradition of the Victorian sage.

O'Malley, Ida B. *Florence Nightingale, 1820–1856: A Study of Her Life Down to the End of the Crimean War*. London: Butterworth, 1931. O'Malley's biography remains very readable, and it contains some correspondence not available elsewhere.

Pickering, George. *The Creative Malady*. New York: Oxford Univ. Press, 1974. Pickering provides a discussion of Nightingale's invalidism.

Poovey, Mary. *Uneven Developments: The Ideological Work of Gender in Mid-Victorian England*. Chicago: Univ. of Chicago Press, 1988. Poovey's chapter on Nightingale's "social construction" examines how her work employs both military and domestic rhetoric.

Rosenberg, Charles E. "Florence Nightingale on Contagion: The Hospital as Moral Universe." In *Healing and History: Essays for Charles Rosen,* ed. Charles E. Rosenberg. New York: Dawson, 1979. Rosenberg discusses Nightingale's ideology of morality for hospitals, nurses, and patients.

Showalter, Elaine. "Miranda and Cassandra: The Discourse of the Feminist Intellectual." In *Tradition and the Talents of Women,* ed. Florence Howe. Urbana: Univ. of Illinois Press, 1991. Showalter presents a useful comparison of Nightingale's and Margaret Fuller's nineteenth-century feminism.

Smith, F. B. *Florence Nightingale: Reputation and Power*. New York: St. Martin's, 1982. Smith's biography is unsympathetic, and its argumentative tone limits its usefulness. However, his research from the Greater London Record Office provides fascinating information on Nightingale's Crimean nurses.

Snyder, Katherine V. "From Novel to Essay: Gender and Revision in Florence Nightingale's 'Cassandra.' " In *The Politics of the Essay: Feminist Perspectives,* ed. Ruth-Ellen Boetcher Joeres and Elizabeth Mittman. Bloomington: Indiana Univ. Press, 1993. Snyder traces the development of "Cassandra" into its final form.

Summers, Anne. *Angels and Citizens: British Women as Military Nurses, 1854–1914*. London: Routledge & Kegan Paul, 1988. Summers places Nightingale's Crimean experiment and her nursing school in the context of the many other nursing projects that were conducted simultaneously, and often with more success.

Woodham-Smith, Cecil. *Florence Nightingale, 1820–1910.* New York: McGraw-Hill, 1951. Reprint, New York: Atheneum, 1983. Woodham-Smith's account is the most accessible and readable Nightingale biography.

Journal Articles

Barrell, John. "Death on the Nile: Fantasy and the Literature of Tourism, 1840–1860." *Essays in Criticism* 41 (1991): 97. Barrell reads Nightingale's letters from Egypt in the context of other tourists' correspondence.
Larson, Janet. "Lady Wrestling for Victorian Soul: Discourse, Gender, and Spirituality in Women's Texts." *Religion and Literature* 23 (1991): 62. Larson examines prophetic speech in Nightingale's "Cassandra."
Pugh, Evelyn L. "Florence Nightingale and J. S. Mill Debate Women's Rights." *Journal of British Studies* 21 (1982): 118–138. Pugh traces Nightingale and Mill's correspondence on suffrage and the nineteenth-century women's movement.
Showalter, Elaine. "Florence Nightingale's Feminist Complaint: Women, Religion, and *Suggestions for Thought.*" *Signs* 6 (1981): 395–412. Showalter provides a useful general introduction to Nightingale's theology.

Index

The Author

Colleen Hobbs received a Ph.D from Rutgers University in 1994. Her dissertation explored Victorian women writers' use of religious themes as a vehicle for social and ideological resistance. She has published articles on Christina Rossetti's devotional prose, on Victorian sisterhoods, and on Mary Shelley's *Frankenstein*.

The Editor

Herbert Sussman is professor of English at Northeastern University. His publications in Victorian literature include *Victorian Masculinities: Manhood and Masculine Poetics in Early Victorian Literature and Art; Fact into Figure: Typology in Carlyle, Ruskin, and the Pre-Raphaelite Brotherhood;* and *Victorians and the Machine: The Literary Response to Technology.*